# THE ASCENSION PROTOCOL

## KEYS FROM THE DRAGONS FOR ACCESSING YOUR DIVINE HUMAN BLUEPRINT

*Araya AnRa*

# THE ASCENSION PROTOCOL

## KEYS FROM THE DRAGONS FOR ACCESSING YOUR DIVINE HUMAN BLUEPRINT

Araya AnRa

Inside cover page info:
The Dragon Within
Copyright © 2025 Araya AnRa
All rights reserved

Cover illustration by Nicolás Alejandro Peña
https://www.instagram.com/amisgaudi.art/
https://www.deviantart.com/amisgaudi

ISBN 13: 979-8-9927733-0-9

OCC033000 BODY, MIND & SPIRIT / Gaia & Earth Energies
OCC011000 BODY, MIND & SPIRIT / Healing / General

Printed in the United States of America

10 9 8 7 6 5 4 3 2

Email: araya@invokehealing.com
Websites: invokehealing.com, dragonwithin.com, theascensionprotocol.com

# Contents

INTRODUCTION ----------------------------------------------------------- 1

*WHAT IS ASCENSION?* ----------------------------------------------- 3

    SOUL SIGNATURE ------------------------------------------ 12

    HEARTSONG ---------------------------------------------- 13

    UNDERSTANDING THE ORIGIN POINT TO
    ENDPOINT COMPLETION, SIMULTANEITY AND
    INCARNATIONAL FRAMEWORKS ------------------ 14

    UNDERSTANDING THE PATH IN SO WE KNOW THE
    PATH OUT ------------------------------------------------- 25

    THE DIVINE HUMAN BLUEPRINT ----------------- 38

*ASCENSION TERMINOLOGY* --------------------------------- 41

    THE ZERO-POINT GATEWAY --------------------- 43

    THE SPACES IN-BETWEEN --------------------------- 45

    PARADOX -------------------------------------------------- 47

    MAGNETISM AND THE LAW OF ATTRACTION ---- 49

    BOUNDLESSNESS AND VASTNESS ---------------- 52

    MICRO AND MACRO -------------------------------- 53

TELEPORTATION------------------------------------ 54

*BODY SHIFTS* - - - - - - - - - - - - - - - - - - - - - - - - - - - - - - - - - - - - - - - - -*57*

STABILIZING MECHANISM------------------------- 60

SHIFT OF THE CHAKRAS FROM LINEAR TO
SPHERICAL -----------------------------------------61

SHIFT OF LOWER 4 BODIES TO UPPER 4 BODIES 64

APPROACHING THE MENTAL AND PHYSICAL BODY
SHIFTS -------------------------------------------- 69

SHIFTING THE MENTAL BODY --------------------- 77

    Perceiving the inversion exercise ------------------------------ 78

    Seeing through the spaces in-between ---------------------- 79

    Tiling of dimensions --------------------------------------------80

    Contemplation --------------------------------------------------- 81

    Stepping into unity ('mersion')-------------------------------- 81

SHIFT FROM CARBON TO SILICA ----------------- 82

OCULAR NERVE SHIFTS AND THE SENSES GOING
SPHERICAL --------------------------------------- 90

OTHER BODY CHANGES ---------------------------91

    The shift of the breath/lungs expanding to operate within 5D 93

CONNECTING TO THE FULLNESS OF OUR SOUL
SELF ----------------------------------------------94


*HEALING TECHNIQUES AND EXERCISES TO MOVE
YOURSELF FORWARD*- - - - - - - - - - - - - - - - - - - - - - - - - - - - - - -*101*

HEALING OF THE INNER ASPECTS - CHILD,
MASCULINE, FEMININE--------------------------- 103

BREATHING PRACTICE----------------------------- 104

HEALING DIS-EASE/ILLNESS/MISALIGNMENTS/
INJURIES IN THE BODY--------------------------- 105

INNER SPACE EXPANSION ----------------------- 107

WORKING IN THE BLACK LIGHT ---------------- 108

PULSE POINT IN THE HEART ------------------- 109

WORKING WITH YOUR CHAKRAS AS THEY GO
SPHERICAL --------------------------------------- 111

MOVING INTO MULTIDIMENSIONALITY ---------- 111

MEDITATING IN THE EYE OF YOUR DRAGON---- 112

DIETARY SHIFTS AND CLEANSES --------------- 112

MOVING AWAY FROM RELIANCE ON AND
LIMITATIONS OF THE 5 PHYSICAL SENSES ----- 113

SOUL LEVEL BRAINSTORMING ------------------ 114

UPDATING THE SPACE AROUND YOU----------- 116

RELEASING SOUL CONTRACTS AND SOUL
BINDINGS --------------------------------------- 116

COMING INTO ALIGNMENT WITH THE HEART'S
DESIRES ----------------------------------------- 117

THE INVISIBLE BOXES AROUND YOU ----------- 121

DISCOVERING THE NUANCES OF JOY ---------- 122

MERGING WITH YOUR HIGHER SELF ----------- 124

PERCEIVING YOUR HIGHER SELF --------------- 125

RECOGNIZING YOUR PARADIGM---------------- 126

ALIGNING TO YOUR PATH----------------------- 127

INSIGHTFUL CHECK-IN -------------------------- 128

VISIONING WITHOUT LIMITS --------------------- 129

CONTEMPLATIONS ----------------------------- 131

THE CONCERNS OVER THOSE 'LEFT BEHIND'-------------133

THE TIME IS NOW ------------------------------- 137

DRAGONS AND OTHER BEINGS ASSISTING THE PROCESS 139

AndaRan Dragons-------------------------------- 142

Arcturan Dragons -------------------------------- 144

Blueprint Architects --------------------------------- 145

Core-Fire Dragons and Solar Lightning Dragons- 145

Deep Earth Dragons (see also Opal and Black Fire Opal Dragons)----------------------------------------- 146

Elemental Dragons ---------------------------------- 147

Eternity Dragons and Infinity Dragons ----------- 147

Flame Dragons -------------------------------------- 148

Infinity Dragons ------------------------------------- 149

Lyrans----------------------------------------------- 149

Matrix Dragons -------------------------------------- 150

Middle Earth Dragons ----------------------------- 150

Opal and Black Fire Opal Dragons (Deep Earth) - 151

Pleiadean Dragons --------------------------------- 151

Primordial Dragon Mother ------------------------- 158

Rainbow Realm Dragons --------------------------- 159

Solar Dragons -------------------------------------- 159

Starlite Dragons ------------------------------------ 160

Sun Dragons --------------------------------------- 160

Unicorns--------------------------------------------- 160

ACKNOWLEDGMENTS ------------------------------- 163

ABOUT THE AUTHOR ------------------------------- 165

*O*ur evolution - Mastery - happens as we come full circle back to what we came in with; being the child but with all of the wisdom gained, the playfulness and connection to the creative spark that flows when we are connected to ourSelf and the Divine. Look at all of the Masters you work with, especially the Dragons… PLAYFUL! It's all practice and all things in your field are just toys.

The ascension process is much like a surfer in a tube. Once the journey starts, the 3D world begins to curl around you, trying to block the light, tighten its hold and smother you. But you have your eye on the light at the end, with total focus, using the building energy of the spiral to catapult you forward and before the gate can close, you allow yourself to drop into full trust that your intention and momentum will push you through. In that moment of total surrender, you get shot out into the light of a whole different landscape.

All is energy. Time and space are vibrational waves, as are you. You are gently moving into a new resonant field, ever closer to *your*

signature/resonance/energypattern/blueprint, whatever synonym resonates for you. In essence, you are merging with your full Light Body. This has been a common term for decades for the Soul level structure at our origin point. The Dragons very clearly corrected this about a year ago as our vibration levels kept rising and we became aware of greater levels of Truth. Alongside information about our own universe and our Soul being the centerpoint of that expanding universe, they were very clear that a more accurate term is Solar Body or Soul-ar body in alignment with the English term for Soul.

As all your cells feel that alignment more and more, they start to resonate with it and this triggers the biological shift to silica (crystalline) and away from polarized electrical fields. Magnetism becomes like to like fields rather than opposites attracting. Matter then dissolves as a structure in our perception and is perceived in its highest resonance blueprint. The journey becomes a moment-to-moment choicepoint from the heart that determines your vector of experience and resonance into fields of "matter" (time and space vectors). You are moving towards your "Diamond State", which is the ability to hold both perspectives simultaneously: individual awareness/all is ONE.

The last five years on the planet have been particularly overflowing with incoming information for us to grasp the process we are entering as we choose ascension. This body of information is the weaving together of all of it into what is hopefully concise, comprehensible, digestible, and cohesive. There may be sections that you have to read multiple times and others that need to percolate in your field for a while before the 'aha' pops through. Stick with it.

As we embark on this journey together, I offer you these keys and codes held and brought forth by the Dragons for the benefit of all of humanity moving through this ascension gateway. What an exciting time to be alive!

# WHAT IS ASCENSION?

We have been throwing around the term 'ascension' for decades now, but what do we truly mean by it? There are some out there touting new planets that we will migrate to. Others feel that it is a migration or movement into something akin to an angelic realm. In my understanding, it is a lot more practical and a lot more simple. Ascension is about increasing in vibration or 'ascending' up a vibrational ladder.

The shift from 3D to 5D is essentially a shift in perspective. We our shifting our vantage point into a higher vibrational plane where more Truth is not only perceptible, but where our telepathic fields are fully open to interact within it from a different basis of both information collected and shared. It requires full transparency of our Being to connect into it and so the path becomes one of opening more and more to full Trust in our own knowing and our higher Self guiding us towards it. When we release all of our traumas, woundings, belief structures and limitations, we can allow the Heart and our full Self to be in transparence.

## THE ASCENSION PROTOCOL

Imagine you are looking straight ahead and you thus see the grids of the universe - your experience of it - in a certain way. If you were to bend forward, those grids would seem to align differently. You may begin to perceive the spaces in-between, the overlays, the intersections. That subtle shift dramatically changes the interaction with that reality field. Now add in emotion and the color fields associated with each and it shifts again. This is why the 'future' from a 3D perspective is uncertain. There are hundreds of potentials, yet one path based on CHOICE in each moment. In 3D, our choices have ramifications that ripple through the entire field of potential. When we fully realize a soul lesson from that choice, we can actually move through the timelines and change or rewrite previous choices which can then affect the 'now'.

Let me give you an example of this. Imagine a lifetime as a sailor in the 1800's, maybe as part of a navy or as a privateer (many of us have chosen a lifetime like this!). During that lifetime, at a port of call, a romance took place and a child, a daughter, resulted. Over the first year or two, there were a few visits, but very infrequent and not much continued interest on your part as the sailor. You took no part in the responsibility for that child by sending funds, clothing or the like. Both mother and child suffered greatly because of this.

Now, in your current life, you begin to experience a similar play out, although from the other side. You would find yourself in a similar energetic dynamic of neglect even if the circumstances aren't identical. This is a karmic balance unfolding. To recognize it, you may have already experienced past life memories in meditations or inner work that start to pop up as you reflect on your current circumstances. It also may be that as you ask for clarity about your current life, that you are shown the past life connections.

You can choose to stay in the suffering and resentment, etc. of the situation OR you can travel through timelines into that field, connecting with yourself as the sailor. You could, as one option, *change* your choices by taking responsibility and being involved in the child's life. Done with clear pure intention and repentance because of recognizing the unloving-ness of the previous choices, the timeline shifts, the soul lesson is learned and the current life playing out also takes a dramatic shift. Done with impure intentions merely to be released of suffering, changes nothing. This is about lesson completion by acknowledging our lower vibrational choices out of alignment with our core essence.

Another way to grasp this is to imagine a radio and the current station you are listening to. The 3D station is full of chaos, fear, challenges, frustrations. When you want to listen to something else, you turn the dial in gentle increments until you find the new signal of a smoother listening experience. This one is peaceful, even magical, but you won't be able to listen to it until you CHOOSE to change the channel and make those little jumps to higher bandwidths to find the new station.

The key to this shift is fluidity. We have to let go of our relativity in perception. We are accustomed to perceiving based on our surroundings, those around us and universal laws of our surroundings that we have come to accept. We perceive in relation to all else rather than as it exists in absolute Truth. What we need is to become in such a state of flow in full connection to the heart, that we allow wherever we are at to be the foundation of OUR perception, without limitation on the field of possibility or potential. A small example of this would be to envision yourself in a sphere and there are bubbles in the sphere. Your current 3D mindset would only allow you to be either in the sphere or in one of the bubbles. Your heart in perceiving this would allow you to be in the sphere AND in a bubble, and the bubble could even be larger than the sphere. The mind cannot allow this. These are the mental body roadblocks that we will come across as we move forward in releasing them all.

We have massive boundaries or blocks in place within our physical, mental, emotional and energy bodies. Our central pillar,

though, is perfectly still and aligned. When we let the massive waves of incoming Light that are helping us get realigned to that central pillar break down the walls, we slowly expand from the center out. Like rock walls on a shoreline, the longer and harder the waves crash against it, eventually they will crumble. As they do, our still core is able to get bigger and bigger.

Another way to look at this shift makes sense to those who have worked with Photoshop or other photo editing software. Instead of being in the 'main' layer (the only layer in 3D), we are opening other layers to experience. Or more accurately, those layers have always been there, but we are now able to make them visible. We also move into the capacity to choose when and how long the background layer of '3D Earth' is visible and whether we want to interact with it or not.

These other vibrational layers have always been there, we have just been veiled from interacting with them. Seeing them as concentric spheres that can at the same time be within and without each other is one way the limited mental body can grasp this idea. In Truth, most of the physics and structure that exist are beyond what our limited capacity can take in. Since the December Solstice of 2023, these spheres have now moved into a state of cohesion, meaning that our sphere is no longer in full separation from them, but can move into synch with them as we choose to.

So our task becomes to shift our perspective point from how we experience reality 'now' to that of 5D or higher. The biggest key to this is being able to move deeply into the heart and allow trust in our Self to build while we break down the belief structures that keep us anchored in this version of reality. We have to redefine or drop definitions of our reality. For example, as we look around us, we often perceive things as either masculine or feminine energetically. What if we allow the other aspect to be seen within it? This simple shift sets the template for Union in our field and these things becoming 5D for us.

Our mental body will fight us on this, as will our senses, because they are the greatest anchors we have to 3D. When we can open the telepathic body and allow ourselves to see, touch, taste, hear, feel and know from the energetic space, we rely less on our physicality and allow it to shift. We currently 'see' the 3D hologram outside of ourselves as our 'external reality'. When we drop through the heart in our communications and begin to experience the hologram from this space, we can acclimate to it and eventually allow it to become our new 'external' reality. A veil will drop behind us at some point of our own choosing, separating us from the old 3rd density layers.

This reality will seem as tangible, although it will be more 'rich' in texture, color, sound pattern, etc. than the current one we experience. Those on the ascension pathway are actually already flitting in and out of this experience, particularly when they reach a state of pure joy. At the soul level, joy is our natural state of Being. So, when we truly experience joy, we naturally align more directly into that higher vibrational perspective state. We don't always take note of the experience, although we can look back on how it felt as though we were transported out of our ordinary life, even momentarily, into a field full of potential where anything felt possible. When we have the realization of the experience, we actually notice while we are in it, the lightness of body, clarity of the field, sounds, and colors around us, and 'less gravity' in both our physicality and emotional state.

Part of this is because we are vibrating at a much higher rate that matches our new surroundings, but we are also lifted into a new set of 'surroundings'. 3D is limited to about 8 octaves. You could also look at these as 'notes', 'strings', 'layers'; like having 8 floors that your elevator can access. 5D has 56!! It has the base 8, but within each of those 7 layers expand which is what allows, for example, an incredible variation in color spectrum that cannot be experienced in 3D. The greatest block your mental body will hold against you moving into this and all experiences within 5D or higher, is that it will shut it down with

the simple concept of 'impossible'. When we can pull the incredibly limiting cap off of what we allow to be possible, we can actually open to the full field of potential and allow creation and manifestations to happen naturally.

A big part of ascension and our awareness of our progress within it, is directly correlated to what we begin to experience as 'instant manifestation'. You are energy. Everything in the universe is pure energy, whether you ascribe a hologram to it or not. If your vibrational rate is increasing, and your blocks or hindrances to 'possible' decreasing, you will naturally begin to experience a heightened electromagnetic field that draws to it matching energies. When you 'create' or intend something within your heart space that would bring you pure joy, the universe naturally responds with the matching energy that is that experience. It might be as simple as what I call 'rock star parking' (front row, short walk to where I want to go, even when super crowded). But, when this starts to happen over and over again, that is when realization dawns of your progression and your remembrance of how the universe actually operates.

One of the easiest ways to connect with our highest vibrational field is to just allow joy. When you are in 'joy', you are in conscious connection with your Soul level. This is how you stay in the 'froth'. The 'froth' is the high point of the wave, the high state of excitement (energy) that *is* your Lightness of Being. That joy pervades the heart, much like bliss pervades the body when you experience it. If we are not in 'joy', something, somewhere within us is not willing to be.

It can be hard to believe that we have to have a willingness to be in joy in every moment. Why would we push joy away? Joy feels so good! Our soul level Self is always in joy, but the belief structures of this realm have squashed that out of us or more accurately distracted us away from it. So, it becomes key to intend this merge with your Soul level Self in every moment. Intention is literally sending a direct signal to another energy field, so intending this merge is the conscious sending of a signal into your higher energy field that you *desire* to connect.

The power of intention is greater than you realize. Don't let rote activities like brushing your teeth, cooking, and driving *not* be moments to be in joy. The goal here is to be so aligned with your True Heart (full Solar/Soul-ar Body merge), that you are creating the reality of your dreams in every moment. And in Truth, this isn't actually a goal, but what we have moved away from in coming to a third density experience and how we were designed to interact with the greater Reality. Are you ready for that? Do you actually believe it possible? You are your own biggest limitation in realizing it.

Can you allow yourself to live in ease, flow, reception and grace? When you are ready to live in that, that is what will exist.

Let's call it Heart Presence rather than ascension, because it is truly in and through the inner gate of the heart that we access our full Self and the 'inversion' or true righting of the ship. We have actually been inverted as a reality all this time. Now we get to return to alignment with the rest of all that exists outside of this tiny blip of a 'reality'. If you want to imagine how small this blip really is, envision an x-axis and y-axis that run to infinity. Call one Time and the other Space. Our entire reality exists in the singular, tiny point of their intersection. Everything else is all that we have been veiled off from and are now opening to.

For most of us, we can't even pinpoint what our heart desires yet. If we individually don't know what we want, how will we be able to hold a collective common vision of what we are creating together? Imagine a potter. He is uninspired and sitting with a lump of clay before him. He pokes at it, pushes it, pulls it... but can't create anything with it until there is an inspiration. In the quiet sitting, the stilling and centering of the heart and mind, the masterpiece reveals itself inside the clay to the heart of the potter. The telepathic communion between their fields was realized and all of a sudden the potter can dive into pulling it out of the clay. We need stillness to get the clarity of the vision - the call of the heart - to what it actually wants to experience and/or create. An important key here is to put energy, not effort into your creations.

We are also entering a unique phase of evolution in that the New Earth truly holds a 'communal' harmonic. All will be co-created together, as it was in its descension, by teams coming from different star systems, galaxies, universes, lineages, etc. Now it will be co-created all from a human commonality. As each individually awakens to their True Self and who they BE, they step into the arena to co-create from the heart with all others who have also reached that point. To create the New Earth, all will share their HeartSong and a piece of each then will infuse into a 'joint' HeartSong that *is* a new creation. Because all are part of it, all will share in the enjoyment of, responsibility for, pride in and maintenance of it.

> # Put energy, not effort into your creations

All it takes to change the game is the set of rules you live by.

## SOUL SIGNATURE

As you begin to reconnect with all that you BE, you will come to recognize and remember your soul signature. Your soul signature is how you are recognized and how you recognize other Beings. For example, when you encounter one of the Ascended Masters in a meditation or dream state, you immediately know who they are because you are energetically recognizing their signature. The signature is comprised of vibration, color, sound, and geometry. It is your unique individuation and characteristics bestowed upon you at the moment of your creation as a Soul by God (Creator /Source). You may find it very different than who you think you are now, because your 'personality' comes from 3D: parenting, friends, socializing, etc. In order to be accepted, you have shifted away from your actual signature and gifts. Your identity in 3D is part of what is keeping you there. What Soul level characteristics are you blocking from expressing?

The beauty in remembering and seeing your Self truly is that it releases condition and allows you to begin to see others and embrace their characteristics and individuation rather than their personality. When you allow them to BE, they can evolve towards ascension and full alignment to themSelves as well. You begin to move to the true state of unconditionality with a full open heart.

An important note here is to not limit what that signature or your core 'form' may be. We often expect (which limits our perception) it to be a recognizable form of Being like Dragon, Angelic, Star Being, Mantid, Fairy, Unicorn, etc. There are Souls created though that are more like the space in-between form. They feel more like backdrop energy, which can be really confusing for our brain because we want to have 'identity' which is 'form'. My first awareness of this was in contact with matrix dragons. They are massive energy fields that very clearly hold signature as Dragon and yet are that backdrop in and through other forms on varying scales. Chaos Dragons, too, are a similar yet subtly different expression whose structure is like energy that's behind pushing other energies forward. The takeaway here is to be fully open to what it may be as you discover your origin and signature.

## HEARTSONG

The HeartSong is the part of your signature that aligns with the pulse of the universe. It is the melody from your creation along

with all of the harmonics of complexity added to it from all of your soul learning. The complexity of the harmonies, like our geometric structure, is added to with each incarnational experience. If it were a symphony, every 'plane' or 'realm' we experience is like adding another instrument, while every incarnation within that plane or realm adds a few more bars or notes. While the Earth realm may be the cello of my HeartSong, it may be the clarinet of yours and the Lyran system might be my lead violin while it is your bass.

Coming into contact with your Heart Song and allowing yourself to connect to it is a powerful opener to the Truth of your Self.

## UNDERSTANDING THE ORIGIN POINT TO ENDPOINT COMPLETION, SIMULTANEITY AND INCARNATIONAL FRAMEWORKS

The journey to full reconnection with Self is what we have embarked upon in this ascension process. For years, it has been my work to assist others in merging with who they BE. Most of those have been of Dragon origin and so I have focused on merging with your Dragon, although it really is the same regardless of what your origin energy is. What I taught and shared as the Way of the DragonHeart was a merge process back into the core of the Heart in order to meet and embody our True Self. What has come into clarity is that what we have actually been in the process of doing is merging our endpoint (where we are in this lowest vibration experience in 3D) back to our origin point. It is in that reconnection, that the loop closes and shifts into a full sphere of conscious embodiment of all aspects of Self.

In many instances we have reached a connection with what we believed was our highest Self, like meeting our Dragon or Angelic aspect. It is now key to go further into yourself, into the origin point. As an example, Jeemla, whom I know as a Dragon King, always presented as an Emerald Dragon, much like my Dragon was always

14

perceived as a Water Dragon. I took that as his form without much more consideration because it was what needed to be the guidepost until we were ready to move beyond it. Then, he encouraged us to go before emerald or actually behind it, within the origin of the emerald that we always perceive; to go further back within the soul level structure.

He pulled me back into that space where I know him as Dragon King and remember when the commanders all unanimously agreed to be in service to this Universe and Gaia's desire to experience a polarized planetary field. He was there as king. and there was something with this energy field that I hadn't taken time in that space to dive into or to notice that he wanted me to see. I kept hearing the word bedrock and feeling a sense of profound depth energetically.

He wanted me to look at profound… profundity in our wording, in our languaging. When you reach a profound space or the concept of profundity, it's like going deep, deep, deep into the bottom of the well. And this is where it's time now to go within. The space of our Truth. As our Soul level merges into our human aspect, and our human to Soul level, we now move into the profundity or the essence and origin point within that. Visualize a boiling pot of water and focusing where you see the bubbles rise from the bottom of the pan when it starts to boil. You can look at the whole pan and see all of the water (our full Akash), even the bubbles (incarnations), but it's really about where the bubbles start.

We have to go much further back in awareness of ourselves and what our structure at soul level actually holds. Coming to know ourselves truly, having the full picture, brings it around us into a full sphere of extension and awareness that neither negates any of the expressions and experiences that are within the sphere, nor between the origin point and the end point. The end point isn't just your last lifetime, but the furthest out extension into density from the very high vibrational octave of the origin point. Your current 3D framework is just the lowest expression there in a linear extension from the origin.

## THE ASCENSION PROTOCOL

The end point comes full circle and embeds into the origin and it becomes where there's knowing of all. We no longer need to even rest within a singular incarnational experience. You move into a space to be able to encompass all aspects of self simultaneously.

This empowers us to release all of our perceived limitations within this incarnational experience. Coming to completion in a system means that you have experienced every single possibility in that system. That means that within your Living Library of knowing, you know how to deal with or balance every single limitation you have designed for your current frame: anxiety, irrational fears, depression, etc. As an example, if you suffer from anxiety currently, some part of your greater incarnational experience in the Earth plane already knows perfectly how to be in pure calm, that all is exactly as you have created it. As you tap into that part of Self, your current mental body can let go of that belief structure.

That's really the ascension process. I've described it as a shift in perspective point. So, it's that perspective point movement to the origin point that allows the encompassing and the embrace of all of the perspective points within where they can actually come into a singular point of awareness. Just don't let that confuse you. If you're listening with the heart, you'll feel all of the expressions that you've been across all dimensions popping up in random moments. These are knowings of you that are embraced by you as aspects and the ability to see the gift within each, regardless of whatever judgment or conditioning may have been on them at an earlier perspective point.

You could envision it like a comic strip full of captions or speech bubbles that spreads across a full little book. You have all of these little speech or caption bubbles and each one of those is not about talking, but it's an expression of us. What shifts is that they're just all in the same frame now instead of being spread out across the comic book. Imagine it was so many pages long and every frame had a little caption bubble. Then you squeeze and pull all of the bubbles into one of the frames. And that frame was both in the middle of the book and yet was the book itself. They are all still visible as individual aspects and yet, because they're all on the same frame, you can feel them energetically all present.

Go ahead and just feel the energy of that field and let information rise. Much of it may surprise you. Most likely, you will feel the proximal ones that are closest to your current bubble of this lifetime, because they are part of the earth plane that's completely wrapped together. But if you feel energetically, you will start to feel pop up all of those between here and there. There may be the sense of multiple different star systems where there are expressions of yourself. The key here is in allowing access to come into all of them simply with full openness in the heart for whatever experience to come into your field of awareness, acknowledging it and just knowing it's present and part of. And if it holds useful information at a given point in the journey, and this is true for any of those journeys, they're now interconnected to be able to use that knowledge and wisdom that each has gained.

Many at this point may wonder about timelines or whether some of those experiences in other systems can be simultaneous. Absolutely. In fact, they're all simultaneous. You have to remember that your frame of reference in 3D holds a linear timeline and so you see things as past, present and future. But, from the other vantage point, it's almost as if they're all unfolding simultaneously. This is hard for your brain to wrap around because they're out in an extension expressing and everything that one does is affecting and enhancing the others.

So you can look at it from your point of history. Let's look, for example, at the Orion wars. They were part of dropping this system, these frames, into duality and down into 3D. We may have been part of that densification process during what happened in the Orion wars and the energy that was pushed forward in waves in order to break that up. And now the energy being pushed forward, in contrast to that, is the unification energy to bring us back into a unified field. So you look at that as history, as something in the past because in the world framework on earth, it's been millions of years since that process. As long as the earth has been around, even millions or billions of years in your frame of reference.

From your soul level vantage point, there is still a kind of time vector that operates in this field, but it's not the same and it's not stretched out in a linear fashion. You could picture it more like a tight spiral. A useful analogy to comprehend time would be to perceive the operation of time as a large bottle with an open end on the base. Time is open or non-fixed within the bottle but like a sequential spiraling. Where the neck of the bottle narrows, 'time' moves into the compression or density of 3D and thus becomes more 'linear' and less 'open'; the timeline becomes constrained.

So there are things that predecess or come before and build on themselves, but it's more simultaneous than you would imagine. There are also more incarnational aspects simultaneously happening than you might imagine. Let's say that there's a bubble of expression over here and it's experiencing all of these things. Those are recorded in your records, your Akash, and so it feels like history. But, because that's an open frame, you can incarnate into it currently and still go in and have that experience.

Think of Atlantis. Atlantis was a period on earth that most of us consider to have been thousands of years ago. Yet, you can still go in and incarnate into that dimensional sphere to have the same historical frame of reference, the same kind of experience and learning that they went through even through the demise at its conclusion. You could almost look at it like dropping into a story book that's on one of your library shelves, but you live it. You go into that frame, you get birthed into it, you have that experience. Your current human self would be recognizing it as memory of Atlantis even though it's happening now. Are you getting a glimpse of what we are talking about?

The easiest way to grasp this is to consider it as an archetype frame that souls can go into for that lesson. Dimensional spheres like Atlantis are spheres of experience. An easy analogy would be to envision a college campus. This building is science. This building is linguistics. This building is mathematics. This building holds the arts. Instead of going into a building for a specific learning, you go into a dimensional sphere that's going to offer specific learning or experiences.

Most believe that Atlantis is done, that it got destroyed because it's in our timeline as being destroyed. But, that dimensional sphere still exists and you can still go into it at any point from how it experienced a beginning to its end. You can also go into multiple points on that 'timeline'. You can incarnate into it as many times as you want to in order to learn everything there is to learn there. Just like going into the science building on campus where you can go in every classroom and learn from every professor. Then, you might move on to something else that's a different discipline. It's a really a useful way to envision how the greater universe operates and from your soul level, the incarnational aspects that you have out there.

Another interesting point to bring in here is that we limit remembrance of our incarnational expressions to what we are willing to recognize. We limit them to body frames, but there are also experiences and lots of learning that happens in frames that would be more like an energetic expression. As an example, incarnating as a Being or consciousness within the sun or within a solar field to experience the pushing and the mechanics of how suns express and constantly push and pull from within to expand energy outward. That's not a normal expression or incarnation you would think possible. There are so many more expressions possible than we've yet been able to perceive. As we open that cap and lift that lid off, you will start to experience, remember and touch in with other ways of "incarnating" or "expressing".

Did you know that you could go in and experience being wind as a consciousness? A solar storm? A galactic field? An asteroid belt?

These are things that we look at as not having consciousness, but they do. They are fields of expression that maybe not as many souls choose to go in and have, but they are open frames of experience. We have to begin looking at the universe and the multiverse beyond it, of all that exists within those, as an open frame for an incarnational experience that you can move into with part of your energy field to experience it.

Some of them are very brief as an encounter: you have it, you can understand that expression and then you pull out of it. That's where there are records within you that are "past" or "future", but in a way they're all there and available right now, which means they're simultaneous, even though you might have done it very early on in your soul's history, so to speak.

> You don't know where your limits are until you see beyond them.

As this information comes into your field, you may feel like your heart and mental bodies are expanding, as if opening up horizons that you didn't know were there. That's always the case. You don't know where your limits are until you see beyond them. That's a profound statement.

Everything that has structure to it, frame to it, is really a form. It's a geometric. It's an energetic that because of its energetic field and the output of that energy, it's seen as form even though we would see it as non-form. This is why we've been challenged to accept or open to the idea of beings in non-form like matrix dragons and chaos dragons, the energetic backdrops of things that are not in form. They are what you would call non-form even though all of those are form because they hold energy. Anything that holds energy has a form, but definitionally, we have a limit or a set of brackets around "form". And so now we're taking that lid off.

All we are doing is very subtly and gently lifting another barrier off that you didn't know was there. There's a boundary around your heart and your mind, that as you move into physical proximity to full engagement in this ascension completion, is an open field. As it comes to its completion, every time we move your emotional body and your mental body up a notch or really open a notch, then it brings the physical body along behind it so that it can begin its subtle shift.

What do you think happens if you pull boundaries and limits off of your mental body? It's automatically, because it's energetically in proximity to your physical body, pulling the limit off your physical body that you did not know was there. That is what will allow more crystalline energy to infuse within it for the biological shifts to start taking place. It's just what follows suit.

As awareness begins to come in of your many incarnational aspects, it is important to give the mental body a greater expansion into the field of possibility as to what you may discover. Each incarnational memory also gives insights and clues to your Soul Signature. Each of us is created with a set of characteristics and a scale of varying degrees of each of those within us, making us each unique creations. In incarnating in different systems, you can choose different characteristics and go into new fields, or repeat fields, from a different ray and that sometimes leads into different forms and experiences because you're focused on something different. What we choose to express as from the soul desire will have to use or be facilitated upon what's within our construct to branch out on. Each time we have to choose one meridian to extend out on.

Let's get a visual aid to grasp this concept of incarnational framework. Visualize an oven rack. The oven rack has silver wires with lots of rows and several crossbars. If all of the rods or bars of that rack were meridians of your soul structure, put yourself at the very middle

and then see where they all branch out. It gets much more convoluted and complex than that, but it gives you a basic structure to wrap your head around as to how they're all interconnected. You can see how you can travel along one particular ray or meridian and break off in a subtly different direction with each choicepoint, with each incarnation that you choose to have by taking form or having experience. We're consistently and constantly building our own road map of our own universe.

We know certain roads really, really well, because we've traveled them a lot, sort of like your neighborhood and the places that you go in town that you visit a lot. You know those roads, you know those routes. And there are other areas in town that you know are there, but you haven't really explored them so much. So it's really very similar with your own soul map you might call it. There's a bunch of constructs and things mapped in, but there's a lot in between them that are fields of potential that are just waiting for the choice to go down them, waiting for the choice to go into that neighborhood, so to speak.

We create it as we go. We're mapping out, quite literally, our own universe because we are each our own universe. When you hear the word universe, you think "oh, the universe is massive. It's got all these stars, all these planets, all this space and it takes light years to get across it." But, you also know that everything exists on a micro scale and a macro scale. The universe is a very large road map of a very large Being or set of Beings that are interacting together, because we can make larger systems when we interact with others. And yet, everything in existence mirrors down to the micro level. So, taking that concept of universe and applying it to yourself and every scale in between is going to bring a lot of insight to you.

When you can understand it on your individual level, that will also give you a lot of insight into the larger actual universe level that is based on the planetary system and all of the planets interacting to create something bigger and the multiverse's universal systems interacting to create something even bigger. You are the creator, the keeper, the master of your own universe and, as has been expressed before, the more experiences we have on soul level, the more complex our geometric structure becomes. Every experience you choose in other structures, is based in your own universe on what rays of experience and characteristics you want to go in and explore of yourself because it's always, at every time, about learning about yourself.

This is what all of creation is. It's God learning about himself, herself. It doesn't matter, as there's no gender. God is not a gender. God is a state of energy. God is a Being and you are no different. Every single experience you have is to learn more about yourself, to love yourself more, to know yourself more and to continually expand.

One of the things that goes hand in hand with that is that every level of complication that is within that geometric, that structure, almost forces an expansion energetically that has to move outward. So you do get bigger and bigger as a Being. Just like a city that has so many roads, apartment structures, home structures and buildings when it first incorporates, that city continues to grow and expand. They call it urban sprawl. If you look at Los Angeles now compared to how it started, it's a lot more complex. There are a lot more meridians, a lot more road maps and that's because it kept having more and more experiences.

So, if you look at your own soul growth, much like a city that keeps expanding and sprawling outwards, it's very similar. That makes larger and larger Beings, but they get to have larger and larger experiences. Maybe at a certain level of Being from one of your rays of characteristics that you want to experience, you go out and get to go into a dimensional sphere of a sun to see what that experience is like. A sun is an archetypal energy that can be moved into for an experience. It's a dimensional framework that is there like a pod of energy that you move into and can experience "Wow, OK. This is what it feels like to be a sun." You have certain experiences there and then you go out,

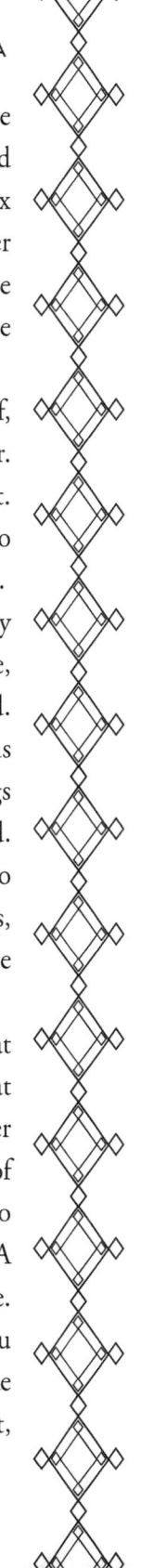

whereas there are other frames in which you actually have a body, a life and all these different things that you're experiencing.

You can really look at it like a game board that has lots of different centers. Every time you choose to, you can expand into a certain number of them at any given time. On a soul level structure we have 144 DNA components. That's the characteristics that you are given at your creation like toggles with meter level amounts of each characteristic that there's infinite number of combinations of. That's what individuates and makes each creation of God so very individual. Then those go out and keep complexifying, keep expanding. You can have simultaneous incarnations and be out experiencing up to the 144 strand capacity.

Let's say, for example, it takes 2 strands to go in and be human, it takes 6 to have a dragon incarnation somewhere and it takes 12 to experience the sun framework. That's how you can have multiple incarnations going on at once. Some do complete and that energetic or that amount of DNA comes back in and then that can go out and express again. There's always a standard amount that is possible. As you're connecting into them from, for example, where we're at with ascension at an origin-point/end-point completion, everything that's been in your experience is available to tap into as your records. Along with that you'll have more concrete or direct connectivity with those that are incarnate simultaneously, that are actually in the experience right now.

I would describe the experience of origin-point to end-point completion as being more expanded, yet more stabilized simultaneously. It is a very grounded feeling, but you will come to a point where you have to change that term because grounded is holding our energy in 3D. Because grounded is really about connecting through the earth, you will find that stabilized is a better word as we expand into the higher crystalline framework of connectivity.

In the past, I would have said, 'Gosh, I feel really grounded' and I'm realizing that it's now not so much grounded as stabilized. There's a very stabilized field, but it's massive. It extends out into this field of vastness that has no limit on it. There's no boundary. It's boundless. And we've known these concepts of boundlessness and vastness that we're moving into. One is on a time continuum and one is on a space continuum, where we go both boundless and then vast. (See Section Boundlessness and Vastness) It's rock solid. And this is where this bedrock energy is.

It's the bedrock. It's the energy from which the bubbles are rising in the pan of boiling water. Take that to a bigger scale. It's the energy at the base of the bubbles rising from the mantle core of Gaia. It's exactly the same frame of reference but on a bigger scale. Then take it bigger to the energy that sits in the backdrop of say a universe from which those bubbles are forming and rising. That's where things are being birthed on all levels of experience.

## UNDERSTANDING THE PATH IN SO WE KNOW THE PATH OUT

There is an inherent principle in the universe known as enfoldment. In order to move into 3D, the structure literally pushed us through a gateway into its flip-side. Our reality seems 'normal' to us, and yet, in Truth, it is inverted. When we move through that gateway in the reverse, it will feel like we are being turned inside-out and upside-down, yet in Truth we will finally be righted. Take note that the movement between 3D and 5D is a conscious choice to move to the other side of the enfoldment and the experience we have will be based on our intention and choice in every moment.

You truly are driving the ship and creating your experience in every moment. You have never been at the mercy of others, never been a victim, never been in an experience other than one that was chosen

and designed BY YOU to have a specific experience. Those experiences may have been soul contracts, karmic balance, lessons... all kinds of things. The fact that you came to Earth at this time, when the ascension process is possible, not only shows a desire to move through that completion point, but that you have completed all of the lessons needed to do so. An Ascension process is only available in any system when one has experienced *everything* that system has available, meaning every role, every emotion... we have played all parts of every story over countless incarnations in order to be able to move forward now and graduate to this next evolution in the system.

A great reminder for you is also the realization that many of those on this path now, that came to Earth to assist at this time, as warriors of Light, are here because they *have* succeeded in other systems where ascension was the next evolutionary process. It is *because* of that Soul level knowledge, that you are here now to help open that pathway for all of the Beings of the Earth plane that at some point will have the opportunity to experience it and evolve when they are ready to do so at the end of future cycles.

We are in a process of reconnecting to origin point on many levels. The further forward we advance, the further back we can reconnect to. One of the big pieces that many remember and have been deeply affected by without realizing it is the history connected to the creation of these lower dimensional planes. The Orion Wars, in particular, hold a deep trauma for all that were connected to it, which is hundreds of thousands of Light Workers. It was a necessary event that embedded the depths of pain and severe loss into the pure hearts of the Dragons and other Galactic Beings that were there for the construction of the lower vibrational planes. They were guarding the etheric templates of Gaia's blueprint and holographic 5D structure.

In order to drop the template vibrationally, the darker emotions of severe loss, shame, guilt, responsibility, separation and the like had to be experienced. It anchored darkness. It was designed to do so. Both sides of the battle knew it was coming and the role they were choosing to play in it. The Dragon guardians, based in unconditional love as a frequency, could only defend, never attack. The Reptilians within the Draco system were those contracted to bring on the attack... to take everything from the Dragons.

That event was the anchoring of the polarized fields that allowed full duality to come into matter. And for many it will be the gateway of healing to remember it and recognize the role it played, very successfully, in the creation of the current system. There is no judgment against those Beings that were the 'perpetrators'. They played a Divine Role. This carries over into our healing in this now version of reality. There are many dark players in roles of perfection, whose turn it is to bring this system to completion by holding those roles until those holding the roles of Light, can embrace them with open, unconditional hearts and merge the two fields back into a state or spiral of Union. Are you ready to do that as one of the Lightbearers?

Recognizing the split of energies to create duality and a polarized field, do you recognize that it then follows to have two paths back to the state of union? Most are familiar with and feel aligned to what we will call the White Light Path. This is the Christ path of right action, more masculine in its approach because it is connected with action, conscious choices, seeking, and learning. There is a comfort in connecting to that brilliant golden-white field of energy and a common starting point for seekers of Truth, spirituality and enlightenment.

The less common path and the one more subconsciously chosen by feminine seekers is the Black Light Path or what we could call the Mary Path. This is the path of the black light, of embrace, of surrender into the void that can be frightening because of its darkness and our subconscious collective fear of the dark and all things within it. There is beauty, softness, potential and the energy of creation within this Void that feels familiar on a deep level. This is the field of potential that we were born of by the spark of the White Light. Most will find

themselves experiencing both paths or spirals to find the state of union at different points of the journey. They are different yet both valid and necessary.

Moving into that spiral of Union requires a bridging from this polarized field to that new field of unity. Many reading this will already have a deep knowing within themselves that they are 'bridges', 'bridge-tenders', 'bridge-builders' or 'bridge-keepers'. They have long felt like they do not fit in, sit within a space where they feel isolated or are between two very different worlds. Each of those that is a part of the Bridge being created takes their place in the scaffolding alongside the 1000's of others that have awakened and stepped forward into their position. This Bridge is built in the energy of true 'community' and is what all of humanity will receive as they cross into the new harmonic.

Many of these 'bridge' Beings have been driven throughout their lives to visit many 'sites' around the world, usually as a deep heart call but without much conscious knowledge of the true reasons for it. As we approach the ascension, they will come to realize that as 'bridges', every one of the sites they visited whether in an awakened state or not, holds an energetic connection to them and also becomes bridged into the New Earth field as they spend more and more time within it. This brings Gaia's full field up into the new and opens those locations as hubs or portals for the communal harmonic to continue expanding and drawing those ready to awaken towards it.

A realization will also dawn that because of the energetic connection to those locations that one has already visited, any grid work, ley line work, portal activations/opening/closing, etc. that rises as part of your Dharmic path, can be done remotely because of your ability to project your energy to that location. You may in fact discover a beautiful symmetry or 'map' that ties all of the locations you 'need' to get to with all of those you have already been to. When you realize the level of Soul guidance you have had all along, even when completely asleep, you turn another corner towards the incredible realization that you are both the player and the game maker. Would this realization change what you begin to create in your life or how you respond to unfolding events? Owning the Truth that you have created every single experience in your life is a huge, empowering step into your Mastery.

## MORE ON THE PATH IN

What I have discovered along this path, is that the further forward I go, the further back I can remember. I have conscious memory of the moment when the Dragon commanders, in the presence of the Dragon King, unanimously agreed to accept the service contract they were invited into to be the keepers of this energetic expansion. Gaia, as a conscious Being, had a desire to experience a planetary embodiment that would be dropped all the way down to a third density field. The Dragons were the perfect Masters to be invited into its creation as they specialize in grids, geometry, large systems and service.

This was the beginning. Many teams were brought in to work in harmony with them to develop this universe and stair-step it down vibrationally from a 12th dimensional outer bandwidth. In its evolution, each step-down entailed the creation of the planet and star systems that would be a part of each vibrational layer. A construction across eons that allowed many incarnational experiences for all of those involved to take bodies in each of those densities and prepare themselves for an eventual third density experience. This allowed for a lot of learning on our parts, but also direct input as the human framework was developed that would allow the Divine Blueprint design of humanity to survive in the conditions being developed for a 3D world of matter.

Many of us have memories of lifetimes in Sirius, Orion, Lyra, Arcturus… in bodies as Dragons, as star Beings, as feline Beings and many more. These were the developmental stages and 'testing' grounds for ideas and concepts for the system being created. You may have memory being triggered as you read this about those lifetimes and the work you were doing there starts to connect into the now.

The dropdown ended up creating a spiral 'elevator shaft' that was the singular path for access into the Earth plane. Any systems on vibrational par with, for example, a 7th dimensional framework, had to access Earth via the Pleiadean system which was holding the 7th, 8th and 9th dimensional platforms connected to this trajectory. The systems within this trajectory are connected to the key Dragon guardians from each that have been present to work with humanity to awaken and move back up the spiral.

| 5D | 6D | 7D - 8D - 9D | 10D | 11D | 12D |
|---|---|---|---|---|---|
| Orion | Sirius | Pleiades | Solaris/Nibiru | Arcturus | Andromeda |

One of the most important pieces of this system sits within the center of the Pleiadean system. (A great deal more is explained in the section about the Pleiadean Dragons.) Within the triple trine of the 9 stars within the Pleiades is housed the Time-Piece Mechanism. This is the structure that allowed the creation of and held in balance the time and space continuums for the eventual third density Earth. The key piece to note here is that everything on the 'lower' vibrational side of this junction was too dense, too slow for our Solar Body to be able to hold its field. This is where our incarnational geometric signature began its slow distortion away from our full Soul level signature.

It became the separation gate at which we had to fully separate from ourSelves and to a degree from our full connection to Mother/Father God that our Solar Body holds. Every experience we incarnated into below the 8th dimension has been at a level of separation. Understanding this energetic separation helps us clearly see the path back to it. It also helps us process and deeply comprehend the full depths of grief we have carried of feeling separate, isolated, lost, homesick, out of place, etc., particularly in the 3rd dimensional realms that are the furthest extension of separation.

After the Orion Wars, with the field of polarity beginning to be created, the Crystalline Core of the planet, held by the Crystal Dragon, took form. This vibrational field splitting allowed the Black and White Dragon energies to pull in opposing directions and fully bifurcate the stream of energy. In the human framework, this allowed for the creation of the Wisdom, Love and Power centers. When we choose to incarnate as 'human', the Soul desire manifests as a spark of energy that, in very basic terms, becomes the Soul Seed that IS the heart center of our Being. It is our full connection to the Divine, our capacity for Love, our pure essence. And it gets dissipated into the body to instill forgetfulness and a veil to our connection.

From the Soul Seed, some of that energy gets pushed downward into what I call the Soul Seat. The Soul Seat is anchored in the center of the Womb/Hara, often referred to as the Dantian, becoming the Power center and the abdominal chakra. The energy of the soul expresses as the womb dragon encased in a crystal sphere. A remnant of our passage through the crystalline core and an encasing of our divine power as creators.

Another piece of that energy pushes upward to form the Wisdom center in the middle of the brain stem/amygdala region. This in turn expands into the 3rd eye chakra. Intuition... wisdom veiled from our true capacity for knowing and hard to access. The beginning of separation.

From here the energy rises in an arc from the power center to the crown, creating the crown chakra and full powerlessness in a state of pure separation from our Divine connection through the heart to Mother/Father God. We are fully dependent on any Divine connection being only realized in a singular incoming direction through the crown. And this only when we seek it out.

The energy from the Wisdom center arcs down and creates the root chakra, pulling us into complete separation from our divine knowing and inherent trust within that to be provided for in all ways. The root, fully separated from Source anchors us in fear and survival instinct.

These are best visualized by looking at the Crystal Dragon symbol that came through many years ago in the writing of The Dragon Within. Admittedly, I didn't even see its full revelations until 11 years later when I began teaching the work in a more in-depth way. The seeds are always there and they bloom when we are ready to see them.

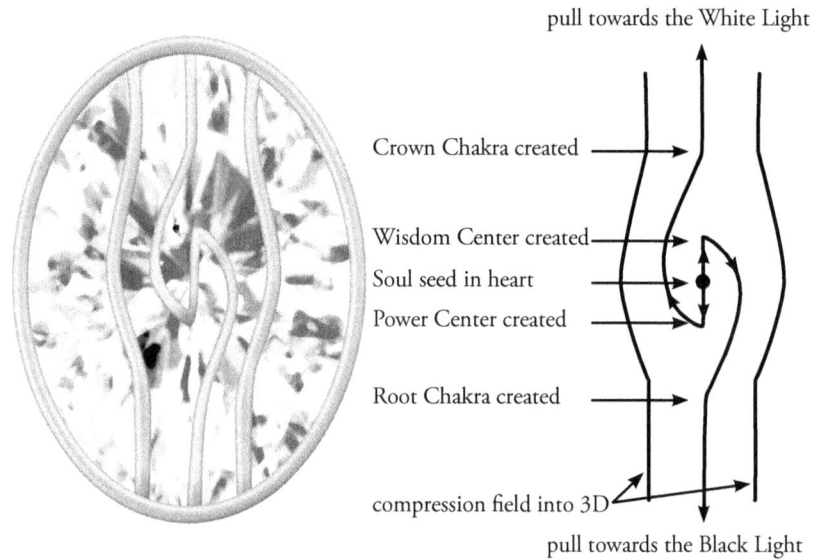

pull towards the White Light

Crown Chakra created

Wisdom Center created

Soul seed in heart

Power Center created

Root Chakra created

compression field into 3D

pull towards the Black Light

Seeing the streams of energy of the Black and White Dragons that pulled that Crystalline core energy apart in order to create the full polarized field of this realm, we have a path home. It is why shadow work, release of trauma held in the body, and examining fully the depths of our own darkness are a critical piece of our awakening. It is the movement back up the stream of the Black Dragon, with his/her help, to the gates of that initial point of pull-apart. The White Dragon stream being equally important: activating the dormant crystalline codes held within us, experiencing our Light and Divinity with his/her help, finding trust and surrender. When these two finally meet at the Gate, we can't help but be drawn into the crystalline field and thus truly begin moving towards the Zero-Point gateway.

## INCEPTION POINT AS PART OF THE PATH IN

A useful awareness tool is to access your memories of your own soul path into this body at this time. By accessing this, you have much more information as to why you designed things certain ways, what contracts you are engaged in, what is left undone and the like. The moment your soul had a desire to incarnate in the Earth plane again is called the inception point. In that instant, a spark of energy like an explosion of creation was expelled from your heart. The very same energy that is the soul seed at the center of your human heart that holds keys to reversing this journey.

That spark of energy first moved along a massive white spiral, flanked by guides with mastery in life construct. This spiral is a path of intention. Staying focused on the intention of the life being created brings all choices and trajectories forward to fine tune as you move along it: height, weight, hair color, socio-economic status, family connections, geographic location, etc. Every step and choicepoint of characteristics leads to direct coding of your DNA.

As these are fine tuned, you move into the spiral of the Galactic Zodiac. As you move along, it determines the geometric match with all planetary alignments for the perfect 'moment' of birth that matches the DNA sequence and geometric soul signature. Once these are aligned, you find yourself on a strip that ends in your 'jump point'. As soon as your energy moves beyond this, the moment of conception is aligned

to and you 'enter' the physical plane. Very gradually over the next 7 1/2 months, you energetically connect in and out of the fetus until you finally 'land' and are continually present for about 6 weeks before birth. This entire period involves the Soul dreaming itself into Being.

The import of this information is that when you can remember that journey and the trajectory, you can move backwards along it to gain invaluable insights and also release things as yet incomplete very quickly. When origin point meets endpoint, loops are closed and spirals can be moved up. You can also reconnect with the depth of Trust you had at that jump point. That level of Trust and surrender to the heart's knowing and desire to move in a certain direction is what will be required for your journey *out* of density.

## MORE ON THE PATH OUT

What is apparent within the information about our path in, is the role the Dragons have played in that expansion. They have been the grid- and code-keepers of this realm and thus hold many keys for our ascension process. All of the information herein has come through them. As Gaia's 5th dimensional New Earth field unfolds and is created by our intentions and rising vibrations, the new grid-keepers are able to step forward. These are the Lyrans.

The Lyrans are most typically feline in form, some being winged like the golden-winged lions. I have encountered Lyrans of all feline form, and many that are feline but not of species we might recognize from those we know in the Earth plane. There are also hybrids within their race. Those I have encountered are Dragon-Lyran cross, but there may be others I have not encountered.

One of the aspects we move into as we raise vibrationally and move into countenance with the energies that they hold, and why they were chosen as the guardians of the next stage of Gaia's evolution, is our 'regal' nature. The Lyrans ARE this regal nature. It is an important foundational energy of the new field and an aspect of dominion, which is one of the two key characteristics of this field. The other is the communal harmonic. As we come into true knowing and alignment (a-lion-ment) with ourSelves, we remember and allow our hearts to open to the harmonic of regality they are holding for us.

In alignment with the true kings and queens of old (we are talking way back... Lemurian and pre-Earth), that regal nature puts the needs of the communal ahead of the individual and provides a seat at the table for everyone. Leadership and governance is aligned to levels of Love within a Being, so it exists, but all are on equal footing to be heard and have input. Masters with fully open hearts are the wise decision-makers once all is presented. All action is based in the heart.

As we progress, you will also begin to experience or connect with more of the Lyran energy and framework and less with the Dragon energy and framework. The Dragons are in the process of handing off their batons of responsibility to the Lyrans. This entails a movement from a trinary or 3-based geometric within the grids to a 4-based geometric that most often presents as 8-pointed stars, cubes or diamond and double-diamond (diamond within diamond) structures in meditations and visualizations. The three pillars of those trines - Love, Wisdom and Power - expand to include the unique pillar of Embrace that the Lyrans hold. The Dragons have been powerful, unconditionally loving beacons in supporting the 3D structure and guiding us towards the next phase of evolution. They now hand off to a field that holds and supports in a field of embrace that envelops us into a communal harmonic.

It is helpful to understand the geometrics of this shift. The Trine is the strongest form in geometry. It is the basis of the grids that the Dragons have held within this universe in order for it to be made manifest all the way down to a polarized field. The trine is created in order to separate from the origin point energy at the apex, yet holds a field steady and allows energetic flow (ether) to move through its midpoint/core.

The new system of the Lyrans that will anchor us into the 5th dimensional field is based on quadratic balance. A 4-based system that creates 8-pointed stars and cubes when those points are joined; the midpoint of both being the tip-to-tip joining of the square-based pyramids that have acted as our merkabah or vessel to travel beyond the 3-D system energetically. As we release lower density energies and come into completion, the bottom pyramid that anchored those lower frequencies moves up through the upper pyramid until the tips are joined and the full axes activate into the 8-pointed star. This re-activates our full Divine Connection Body through the heart center and we begin radiating Starphire (see Divine Human Blueprint section). This open-ended configuration also allows the communal harmonic configuration that we are moving into as it allows connection to everything.

The progression of our configuration

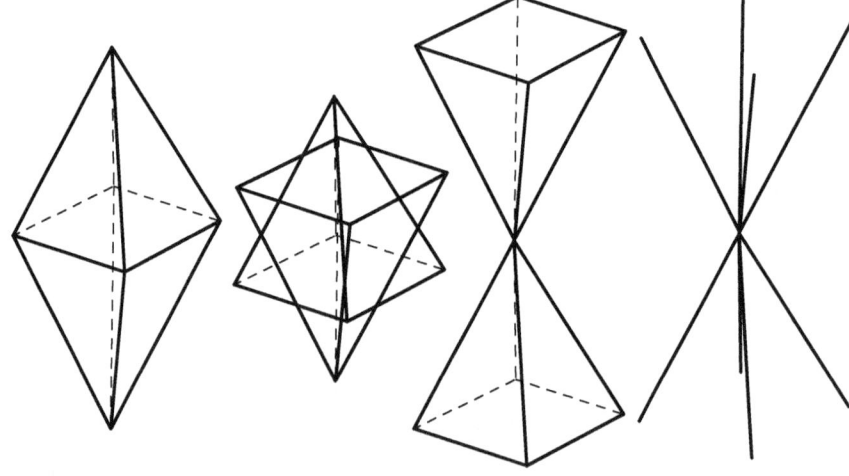

The merkabah itself in its 'diamond' form as vessel, is the basis of our connection to this realm. It holds 12 trines - 4 in the upper pyramid, 4 in the central plane and 4 in the lower pyramid - all connected to the central core; the consistent 12 around 1 construction of the Dragons' trinary systems. Expanded out by the Black and White Dragons from the Crystalline core, this created the field of polarization and our resulting duality. From there, the bringing in of the Elemental Energies stabilized us into the field of matter. In the same way on a micro scale, through the center point of that diamond Merkabah, our 'Soul Seed', the emanation from our 'Solar (Soul-ar) body' (aka Light Body), our incarnational fractal expanded towards both apexes, then was able to stabilize into the elemental field.

The expansion of our merkabah into 3D

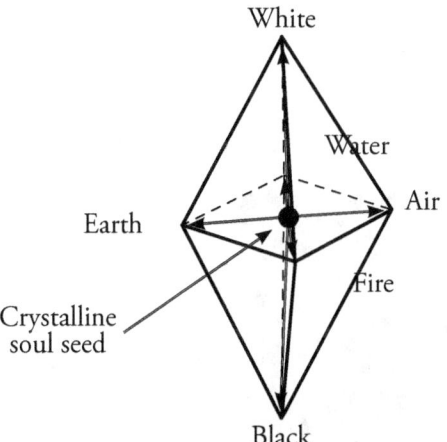

As we shift out of the need for this construct, our heart becomes the center point of the 8-pointed star configuration that allows our interconnection within the communal harmonic as the structure is open rather than closed.

## THE DIVINE HUMAN BLUEPRINT

Humanity was originally created to have a perfect form that could self-sustain, live as long as desired and be in alignment with its environment. Part of the creation and design of each lower dimensional realm involved designing, testing and perfecting an organic format that would fit these parameters as well as the elemental combinations that would support the atmosphere, elemental plane and other creations that would be part of the lowest dimensional plane attainable. The goal was a polarized field in a third dimensional format.

The original architecture and design of the human format was created by a team of specialists in blueprinting from many lineages and systems. With the intention of this system to be the highest form of communal harmonic accessible, it had to be a configuration that any lineage could access and use to have a human experience. It is both the form that the first 'humans' coming into Lemuria descended from and that which we are moving into as we complete our ascension.

This blueprint holds our highest potential form and its core frequency or energy is blue Starphire. Blue Starphire is crystalline energy inherent within our blueprints that actuates into perpetual motion resulting in full ascension capacity. Starphire is the Truth of what you come from NOT stardust! Dust is the fire (phire) that has stopped moving. Starphire is what allows you to become Living Light. All of creation has this core building block within individual signature or geometry in common that is/holds the connection to our Creator. It is our commonality and

> Starphire is the Truth of what you come from NOT stardust!

one of the reasons we can experience 'Oneness' once we reconnect with it.

The constant infusion of Light into our system as we continue to expand our consciousness creates, activates and opens the new chakras in the human body that are at the intersection points of the current chakras. The Human Blueprint has 22 chakras which allows a much higher light quotient to be embodied. This is a more cohesive unit by design which allows greater complexity of geometric configuration to be operational. Activation of these chakras will begin the changes for the biological ascension of the physical body. It is also associated with the increased color spectrum we will be able to experience with the telepathic body.

Full embodiment is the full expansion of Starphire through the Soul Seed in the Heart and the step beyond "merging" with your Solar (Soul-ar) Body. All systems are in full alignment with the Blueprint and Starphire begins to expand from the core outward filling the whole system. This is the micro mirror of the Sun radiating outward filling the universal system. You are the Sun of your universe when fully embodied.

Knowing the field would polarize, the highest blueprint for humanity sits within the 5th dimensional template where it is held waiting for our evolution back into it. The Galactic Blue Beings are actually the galactic level masters (similar to the ascended masters who have acted as guides to wake us up to our Light, but at a higher level) holding the template of the human blueprint for us to attain. They sit within that field of potential as guardians of it. They hold the same Living Light of actuated Starphire within their Beings and its essence is perceived by us from this perspective as part of the blue ray or spectrum. I always laugh in thinking about the moment they first came into my field because they laughed heartily as the message came through 'why do you think it is called a 'blue'-print? I also realized how funny or odd it is that in architecture on Earth, we actually also

call architectural designs blueprints and they even used to be printed on blue paper!

Early civilizations before the densest eras on Earth initially came in with a form very close to the blueprint. Lemurians, for example, were quite etheric in a way because of their proximity to it. They were able to teleport and live thousands of years. They were also much more directly connected to Gaia. The Atlanteans were a step down from that. When you connect in with memories from those eras, if you were incarnate within them, will give you some insight on these differences.

The key now is to be aware that we have a blueprint in alignment with the Divine that can be called our Divine Human Blueprint. It is the structure that holds our greatest potential and the original intention of humanity's role in this realm. As we come in contact with our Starphire energy, we also begin to access our own Living Library in which storehouses of energy are also Living Light. This allows this storehouse of all topics within our soul mastery to rise within us. It is that 'knowing' that comes in as we merge into our full Self.

As an exercise hold the intention in mediation to pull up into your Divine Blueprint and perceive what happens in your body. Starphire is a scintillating energy.

There is more about the specifics of its capacities in the section on Ocular Nerve Shifts.

# *ASCENSION* TERMINOLOGY

## THE ZERO-POINT GATEWAY

*T*he Zero-Point Gateway is the transition point to our ascension, like a gate we pass through from this third dimensional reality into a greater fifth dimensional reality. It is the point in the middle of the coin within which you can touch both sides and yet are not present within either, but also can choose to be in either. In true paradoxical fashion, it is a singularity and yet exists in every centerpoint we are aligned with: the core of the heart, the high heart, the wisdom center, the dantian, the eye, yet also the core of each cell, the core of the planet…black holes at universe level.

As we move into the gate and stand in the middle between worlds, both sides will merge into the center and the sphere of union will expand out around us. This is similar to a toroid field in which you are both at the centerpoint and every point along the outer trajectory

simultaneously. Just allow the mental body to surrender to this concept as it can be a very challenging one from the 3D perspective and understanding of physics. The heart knows and remembers metaphysics so let this remembrance blossom up and through the heart.

To move through it, this gateway literally requires a 'zeroing out'. We walk through it with no baggage… no soul contracts… no karma left to balance… no wounds left unreleased. As we reach certain stages of our evolution and vibrational up-leveling, we come to a point where we realize that anything that is left is now open to be zeroed out through forgiveness and repentance. Any debts we owe, we send out an intention and true heart desire in full repentance to be forgiven of those. Any debts owed us, we allow to be truly and fully forgiven. Any soul contracts still active, we can choose to renegotiate and allow them to be reconstructed with other souls for completion. They can also be fully released and re-engaged from a higher perspective if needed, desired or agreed upon. Soul contracts can hold expectation and keep either soul or both stuck. By breaking/releasing them all, all parties are allowed to shift more into the Truth of who they BE.

This allows all karmic wheels to complete and merge. Much like flattening layers in an application like Photoshop, all of the history of all incarnations in this Earth plane become coded into our Akash. You can imagine this like files and information being stored into a disc or USB stick drive. You don't have to carry it around in the hard drive anymore. It moves directly into your Soul's Akashic records and frees up your field like erasing a hard drive to start again in a new level of experience. It allows a new operating system to be installed. This will begin as you move through the zero-point gateway and into the fifth-dimensional reality. Even 'time' as we understand it is like a clock resetting itself.

Those moving through the zero-point gateway are 'unplugging' themselves from the time-space continuum. Those moving through it and disconnecting are what has been creating the 'warps' and shifts in how we have been experiencing time since the process began. Have you noticed the shifts in your relationship with 'time' or how it operates? It has definitely been shifting. The more that 'unplug', the less stable it is as a field.

Besides an upleveling in vibration and intention to move into a 5D experience, there are several keys to move into and through the zero-point, one being a deep appreciation of every aspect of this 3D physicality. Loving it so much that we can let it go. One of the other parameters is that in order to go through an ascension, you have to have experienced life in a field of polarity. There are so many different polarized experiences: the victim, the perpetrator, the king, the pauper… all the different levels of experience that are possible. We have to have actually experienced all of them in order to zero out and move into an ascension process. This would explain why most of us have had many, many lifetimes in this plane of reality, in order to come in and do that from a human perspective. You have to have that level of achievement or level of completion.

This is why many people feel that they are completing multiple lifetimes of karmic balancing and contracts in this lifetime that falls in the opportunity window for an ascension cycle. I have come across many lightworkers that are on a fast track this time around. There are so many things they are getting done that weren't complete from other lifetimes or maybe an opportunity got missed because their free will was taken away in certain situations. It can feel as if they are living not just multiple chapters in the book of their life, but almost like separate books or short stories within the book because each chapter is so different from the others.

## THE SPACES IN-BETWEEN

When we contemplate the spaces in-between or the interstitial space, we come to know that they are a path to Self, because they are

also the access point to our full merge with our Solar Body and to the inversion of this reality via the Zero-Point. What are the spaces in-between? The easiest way to visualize and understand this concept is to close your eyes and imagine all of the space in and around all of your molecular structure. Science says that roughly 95% of all that exists is unexplainable, incomprehensible 'dark matter' or 'space'. This is true in your body as well. Imagine that your system is a mini universe. Your focus is to become fully aware of all of that space within you. These are the spaces in-between. And this is the most expedient path to experience a full merge with your Solar Body.

I have always explained it in terms of Dragons, because I am a Dragon at my Soul Level structure and my work has been focused on awakening the Dragons. This applies to all soul structures though. So, if you are aware of your soul structure, visualize that in place of 'Dragon' in this exercise. If you aren't aware, just be open and you may remember more of your origin structure.

Sitting quietly, visualize the space or anti-matter in, around and between your field of 'matter' that is your body, cells, bones, etc. Then, invite your Dragon to move up through the spaces in-between into your field. Because the solar body can easily fill this space, you will experience a feeling as if you are overlaid by or within this larger structure; as if you are inside a massive Dragon, or they are within you (or both simultaneously!) Then intend to move through those spaces with your consciousness up into your Dragon through their spaces in-between. Try it in both directions. This allows a deep bodily experience of your full soul structure and may be the first awareness of 'feeling' the horns, protrusions, wings, talons, snout, tail, etc. of your Dragon Self or similar characteristics of your Angelic Self, Fairy Self, Centaur Self, etc. (See exercise 'Merging with your Higher Self')

# PARADOX

The great gift of life on planet Earth is the incredible spectrum of emotion available here. There are emotions to varying degrees in other systems, but nothing like Earth. This is a major reason so many choose to incarnate here. Not only is it a true gem of beauty on an experiential level, but it allows so much growth and expansion on a Soul level because of the emotional spectrum. Our emotions when we fully embrace all of them, lead us to a fully human experience. They are in fact the 'inside out' of each other; a fully human experience results from the embracing of *every* emotion and vice versa. Each is a doorway to the other.

Interestingly, the more we merge into our full Selves, the more fully human we become as well. One might imagine that merging with our Solar Body would make us less 'human' and rather more 'divine', but it is the opposite. The more divine we become, the more joy we find in the human expression and begin to live in the constant natural state of joy, which finds marvel in the baseness of this plane of reality. The desire to leave it behind, plummets us into its fullness. A true paradox.

This idea of two Truths, seemingly opposed, being able to both be true without having to negate the other, is the essence of paradox. It is also one of the Universal principles of the greater reality. In duality, we are naturally aligned to only allowing one Truth. We have to sit on one side of the pendulum or the other.... until we approach the central core and the state of union. It is a natural evolution that comes into your realization as you progress vibrationally towards unity consciousness (or the ascension perspective point). Paradox begins presenting on many fronts of your life, along with a deep acceptance and knowing of its existence. You are no longer forced to choose sides, argue, or compromise. Allowance moves in, which brings serenity, deep peace and knowing. You are beginning to be in connection with your True Self.

## THE ASCENSION PROTOCOL

You begin to walk within the paradox of power in which you become a pillar of strength and clarity, within the softness of grace and divinity. As we sit in this 'synthesis' of paradox, our brain begins to understand it and release all polarized beliefs and paradigms. It allows us to 'see' Truth and move into the full stabilized trine or trinity and away from existing only at the base of the triangle within a polarized field. We bring both sides of duality into a state of unity where we open the heart fully and receive God. It is in this moment that the "Reverie of God" (being made in his/her image only) becomes the "Truth of God" (Being *of* God - a creation or extension of that Divine energy). It is this magical point of inversion that we move into our full crystalline nature and part of the communal harmonic that is the basis of all higher vibrational platforms.

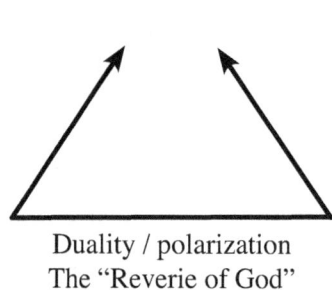

Duality / polarization
The "Reverie of God"

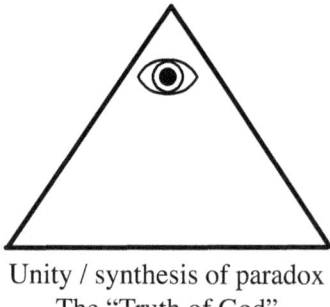

Unity / synthesis of paradox
The "Truth of God"

The return to unity (top of the trine) is the return to 'pure knowing'; to full holographic vision (the eye at the top of the pyramid) or "seeing" from the centerpoint of the heart (the soul seed).

# MAGNETISM AND THE LAW OF ATTRACTION

Visualize a bodhisattva sitting with butterflies covering his hands. His very simple lesson: 'when you become the butterfly, the butterflies will come to you'.

There has been a lot of discussion in the past two decades about the law of attraction and how to enhance it, manifest things into your life, etc. It isn't just about what we can bring in though, and definitely not about using it to our advantage as many would have you believe. It is a quite literal universal law based on magnetism. When you vibrate at a specific frequency, high or low, you will draw to you like frequencies. Thus, why, as an example, when you still have specific limiting beliefs in your field, you will create or draw to you its match. If I believe I am unlucky, I will never win anything. If I believe at my core that relationships are toxic, I will either not experience relationships or attract a toxic one. It is because I hold those vibrational patterns within me and like attracts like.

There is a common saying that opposites attract. Don't let this confuse you about the law of attraction operating in your life. In the realm of relationship in which this saying operates, we do indeed attract, or more accurately subconsciously seek out, that which would balance us as we are *not* in balance within ourselves. This can be with romantic partners, business partners, friendships... any relationships with other conscious Beings. We seek balance externally. We can get stuck in this pattern, which is co-dependence. When we are growing and expanding, we typically recognize that this relationship, unless our partner is also growing into self-balance, begins to stagnate or feel limiting and we seek something different. When we come into balance, we will attract that perfect reflection, either in a new partner or the growth of our current partner.

Your law of attraction is working perfectly in every moment to reflect back to you a perfect mirror of yourself! It is based on the *energy* in your bodies, so includes your emotional and mental body structures. This is what you can use to your advantage to move forward on your path. Most often, people are focused on the law of attraction and trying to create or draw things to themselves with intention, visualization, etc. This can be effective, but if your core beliefs don't support it, whatever you draw in will be fleeting.

The same law of attraction in higher planes *is* operational here, but do we see it? Are we aware and conscious of what that law is trying to show us on a daily basis? What situations are arising around you that you aren't realizing hold a lot more information? Usually these are things that hit us emotionally and not in a good way. Let's look at some examples:

Being cut off in traffic. This upsets you. You might yell at the other driver, complain to others in the car, find yourself in a huff… the gift here is that emotional response. If you can see it as the universe trying to show you something, you will release something and raise your consciousness level (vibration). The key is to actually feel it fully without projecting it at anyone else, most particularly that other driver who is quite literally totally unaware of what they have created for you. They are just God's beautiful messenger because of the creation and application of the Law of Attraction in this universe.

When you dive into the emotion, you might find that it actually upset you, not because of the potential of an accident, making you late, etc, but because he didn't even see you or acknowledge your presence. Maybe a deeper sadness lies under that upset because you weren't seen in childhood. Your needs weren't considered or taken into account. Maybe it brought up fear. Is the fear of getting hit by another car only about that or is there a deeper energetic trying to be seen of feeling unsafe, that control is out of your hands of a situation… there are a myriad of possibilities. What I can guarantee is that once you actually touch it consciously and feel that deeper sadness, fear, lack of control, etc, drivers will no longer cut you off in traffic. If they do, you will be absolutely unaffected by it. Your law of attraction changes based on your energy field that no longer holds a match to a trigger by such an event.

What about something a little harder to see. Imagine your plumbing is clogged up or maybe even the opposite, it sprung a massive leak. Our emotional bodies are all about the water element within us and when we aren't letting ourselves truly feel things or are overly emotional and staying on the surface level of those emotions, this is a way it can be mirrored in your environment. Pent up emotion can literally burst your pipes!

If these things happen multiple times or ways within a short time frame, your higher Self is really trying to get your attention about it. I recall having three separate pairs of shoes - boots, walking shoes and sandals - all blow their soles within days of each other. I was being put on notice that I was not paying close enough attention to the foundation I was laying for myself in a particular area of my life.

One of my clients years back had a really bad mold issue in the walls of their home that wasn't discovered until they were trying to sell it. Direct message: in trying to shift and move forward, he needed to address some very long standing pent up emotional baggage and wounds that were literally seeping in the walls of the house and growing mold.

It can feel overwhelming to start recognizing all the mirrors around us in our life. This is our perfect law of attraction at work. And just like everything else, it isn't a race to the finish and there isn't a need to 'get it all' today, or even this year. Every single crumb you can finally see is a step towards your conscious, ascended Self. Enjoy the journey and let it become a joyous game. Your life is a movie and your Soul is the script writer trying to lead you to the perfect ending.

## BOUNDLESSNESS AND VASTNESS

One of the key markers of our shift into Light is the movement to boundlessness as an experience on all levels. BOUNDLESSNESS is a pull into alignment with the micro and macro of all of creation; to be consciously aware of the full spectrum from the God level (Oneness) to the atomic level. Our core of Light becomes so bright, our field so strong and clear in its output, that our 'boundary' can dissolve. There is no longer a need to 'protect' or have a boundary that separates us (individuation).

The next step is VASTNESS. Once we can release our boundary, we move into a field without limit in any direction. They are two sides of the same coin, but you can't get to the experience of vastness without first moving into boundlessness. It is like stepping into a new arena and once there you realize it extends infinitely in all directions.

This experience is also not only with the energy body, although that is the first place we notice it. The emotional, mental and physical bodies will follow. Just contemplating these allows them to open another degree:

boundlessness in emotions - the capacity to feel the entire emotional spectrum without projection onto others. True unconditionality for self and others

boundlessness in the mental body - possibility thinking with no restrictions, endless creativity! No limits

boundlessness in the 'physical' body - unconfined by the field of matter, density and gravity, what would you be capable of? Living in the Divine Blueprint Body

What are the parameters? And what do you allow them to be? Magic and miracle are part of reality when you allow them to be. Moving into the greater reality outside the limited sphere of the one we have been confined within means the set rules of engagement no longer apply to you!

## MICRO AND MACRO

Gaia too is going through the same evolutionary ascension process on a macro scale. What do I mean by that? The idea of micro and macro or mirroring is a really helpful tool for insight. Everything, literally everything that is happening in your life is mirrored in a micro way down into the cellular level and atomic level and in a macro way up to the planetary, cosmic, galactic, universal and multiverse levels.

That can be hard to imagine, but once you start seeing the correlations, you begin to recognize patterns happening on bigger scales that you can mirror down to yourself and get some good insight. You can also use what you recognize happening for you and see it playing out on the larger scales.

As an example, several years back when the solar flares began to increase, our journey of expansion began in earnest. We were going through big energetic expansions that were allowing our energy bodies to be larger. At the same time, Gaia was also receiving this expansion and quite literally her 'crust' began to break open to allow the expansion resulting in rifts opening in over 50 locations globally within a several month period.

Similarly, her crystalline core activation was beginning as the first humans were activating and opening to their crystalline core pillar. This had effect on a cellular level within us as well as a galactic core activation for its up-leveling.

A really interesting point to contemplate is that macro scale of multiple incarnations. We as humans, have memories of many other lifetimes in forms as other humans, star beings, dragons, tree spirits, angels, fairies, etc. Think of a consciousness like Gaia that also has incarnational experiences, but is a much larger Being. Have you ever considered all of the different planets that Gaia has 'incarnated' as?

# TELEPORTATION

I want to include a discussion of teleportation as I have long felt I would remember how to during this lifetime. I want to share the keys and codes I have received and remembered so far in the hopes that some of you will be triggered into remembering more pieces and help us bring this gift back fully.

There are 3 components to teleportation: telemetry, cognizance and intention.

Telemetry in this realm is defined as the process of recording and transmitting the readings of instruments, especially from remote points. When this term came through it was connected to the energy of geometric and vibrational mirroring. Very similar to the concept of a tesseract, as portrayed in the film A Wrinkle in Time, this component is about knowing the coordinates of your destination beyond what we would know in this world as a GPS coordinate showing longitude and latitude. We are currently limited by our belief structures about and reliance on these 2-dimensional coordinates. When we want to teleport to another 'location', we need to know its full energetic coordinates that also have geometric and vibrational components. In the same way that we as beings have a Soul signature, every 'location' has a similar signature that we need to know fully. What we are missing is the HeartSong or pulse information of the destinations, as well as the larger geometric coordinates in the expanded dimensional planes.

Cognizance. This entails full trust and knowing with full conscious awareness of your destination, your desire to go there, and your successful arrival there. It is a component that operates beyond the singularity of time and can hold an extended frame around the complete journey.

The final component is intention. Full clear intention is required to align precisely to the desired coordinates. As you align your own energy field to the destination field, your local energy field begins to open and release you from it, creating a bridge that will be a moving field of energy that envelops you and pulls you towards the destination.

Part of why we have not been able to do this in the Earth plane involves our cellular structure as well as the Diamond merkabah vessel that we have had to use for 'travel'. The merkabah does not align to the doorways created between vibrational fields of the locale and the destination. When the two spherical energy fields come into proximity via the energetic bridge, the gateway between them is actually the vesica pisces created where they meet. This doorway is like a softened merkabah, meaning in balance with the full divine feminine aspect or in a state of union. Thus, this level of union is another requirement of successful teleportation.

An aspect of that state of union is connected to our cellular structure. As we move into a unified state and its higher vibration, our cell structure moves away from carbon and towards silica (crystalline). The silica state in the body is also required because it allows the ability to align each cell into a unified intention to the pulse of the signature destination. Beyond just our conscious intention, when we have a full crystalline network in place, that intention is amplified into each cell within the 'physical' body creating the full field of unified intention necessary to move every cell through the tesseract into the field of the destination point.

This also brings up the concept of Energetic Morphology. Essentially, this is the ability to restring codes into a subtly different dialect that can then operate within a different field. If we can reawaken that capacity within us, it is purely a matter of restringing our code (DNA) to align to a different dimensional field. This is what we are doing as we incorporate more and more Light and alignment to our actual Soul codes.

# BODY SHIFTS

# BODY SHIFTS

An important aspect of the body shifts you will begin to go through in the ascension process is that all progress will be NON-LINEAR. It may feel at times like you are a pinball going here, there and everywhere without a logical path or order to things. That is exactly what breaking out of the matrix requires. We are stuck in 'linear progression' as a by-product of this polarized field. It is NOT the norm within the greater reality or how we naturally operate. So, to break free of it, your guides and higher Self will begin to bring you into a true flow in alignment with YOUR SOUL, its needs and its most aligned 'order' of things.

Also of note is that no two paths will be exactly the same. What you have to release or embody is unique and different to all those around you. There are similarities, of course, which is why this body of information is being presented. But, your unique Soul signature and sets of experiences set you apart.

## STABILIZING MECHANISM

Historically, as humanity has come into an awareness of itself and connected to higher energies, there has been a need to 'ground' into the physical plane. There are many grounding techniques out there, most often using some method of 'rooting' yourself into Gaia, into the Earth, in order to feel anchored, connected, and stable. As we shift systems, we are uprooting ourselves from 3D and thus our grounding is no longer connected with this anchor or 'central pillar' that is singular, structural, safe and isolated.

The old techniques actually become a hindrance to our expansion, much like we will learn later about how our 5 senses actually keep us anchored or stuck in 3D. New 'grounding' techniques thus need to come forward. As the Earth shifts into its 5D structure, what we start to perceive is the expansion of her crystalline core out to the surface. So, our 'grounding' becomes more like plugging in to a crystalline network that extends out below and around us like a massive snowflake. You could also visualize this like the roots of trees, but they are not 'wood', but crystalline and interweave and connect all the way around the globe and down to the core. A better term for this is 'stabilizing' as we connect into her in a more symbiotic way and stabilize our field within the higher vibrational network. As we stabilize, we find our place within it.

This is the interlacing network that is the foundation of the new communal harmonic of 5D. As we connect or plug ourselves into it, we are required to be transparent, open, and centered in the heart. We then can be part of this grand network and both give to and receive from it. Transparency is a vital component of a communal harmonic. This crystalline network is a pure conductor, as are we when we are fully aligned and merged with our Solar Bodies.

Your heart already knows how to connect into this network, but the first couple of times it may feel odd. Instead of feeling roots grow from your feet deep into the ground, or laying back into Gaia's hands, or maybe even dropping your dragon tail down into the earth to feel grounded, stable and secure, start playing with feeling your own crystalline network connect into Gaia's. Do so by allowing the Light from your Heart to extend out through all of your energy meridians as you feel her crystalline network light up as you connect into it. It is a more electrical experience which we need to get accustomed to as our light quotient increases and our electromagnetic field amps up. We are in fact pure energy, so this journey will entail a great number of 'electrical' ramp ups and higher levels of incoming energies to integrate.

## SHIFT OF THE CHAKRAS FROM LINEAR TO SPHERICAL

Everything in all systems is moving away from a linear format which only predominates in a dualistic system. Our body will go through many changes, one of the first being the shift of your chakras from linear to spherical. If you have worked with your chakras, as most have at this point in their journey, you have known them to be energy centers with funnel like openings from the center point in the midline of your body outward to the front and back or from the crown upward and the root downward.

As these begin to shift, they move away from the linear funnel and pop into a spherical energy center. Each of the 7 main chakras then comes into contact with the others initially in a vertical linear arrangement. This creates vesica pisces shaped crossover zones between each sphere. These zones become amped up or doubled in frequency and start to receive and transmit information in a more direct way. This is the early development of your telepathic body coming online (more on that to come) and your higher capacities for movement of energy.

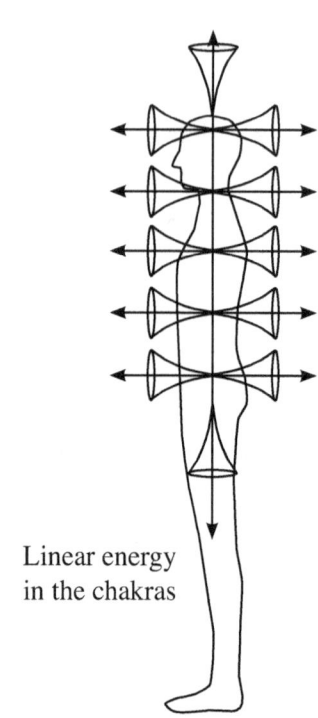

Linear energy
in the chakras

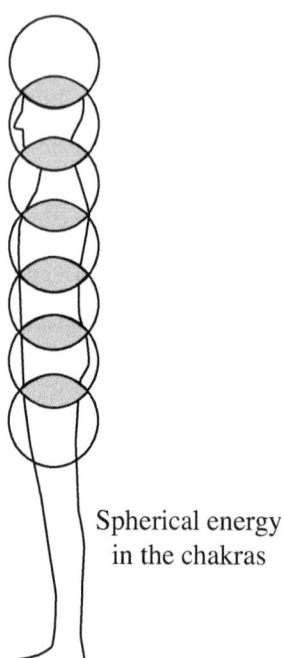

Spherical energy
in the chakras

As the process continues, you will start to notice subtleties indicating that they have moved from a vertical linear formation to something more akin to something like a flower of life. This has an odd sensation of the root being the crown, the crown the root, the heart in the abdomen… essentially all 7 are interconnecting in a pattern that our human brains as yet can't quite grasp. Each of the 7 spheres is connected to all others and yet maintains its centerpoint where the original chakra is in the body. One of the noteworthy aspects of this is that the 'survival instinct' and fears surrounding it in the root chakra are no longer part of your field. This allows you to move into Divine Flow and Divine Birthright in your consciousness.

This is one of those concepts you will start to see mirror into the micro and macro levels as your awareness expands to meet the higher Truths of the universe and multiverse. Many have either not given much thought to the magnitude of shift we are undergoing to move from 3D to 5D, or have misunderstood where we are headed. If you can imagine for a minute, the incredible shift something undergoes between 2D (visualize a flat drawing) and 3D (how that drawing pops out into that 3rd axis), you realize what a huge adjustment that was. It is exactly the same going up to 5D, except that our minds have a hard time conceptualizing that same object now popping both internally and externally in every direction which is what the next leap does.

We are not just walking through a doorway into a higher frequency realm like our energy bodies have been able to experience in deep meditations. Our physical body has some big changes coming. But, the beauty is that we move into each phase of the shift as we are ready, as we intend and allow it and in perfect succession for the transition. It isn't an overnight leap or something we won't be ready for. Remember, YOU are guiding your own process!

## KNOWING THAT ALLOWANCE CANNOT EXIST IN THE SAME FIELD AS RESISTANCE, CAN YOU DROP ALL RESISTANCE?

Another point to take note of here is the movement away from 'linear' to 'spherical' is an energetic movement from rigidity to flow and this will apply across all aspects of the ascension process. External energies that are not aligned to these internal shifts can slow the process. For example, being surrounded by rigidity in form (the architecture around you) creates an energetic of rigidity and more masculine structure in the field. If we are trying to move into more flow, more balance of feminine and masculine energies, it may be beneficial to consider our surroundings and whether or not they are supporting our journey. How can I soften the rigid square construction of my home, office, car, etc.? Even using fabric or scarves to break up the hard corners and edges can help to bring a balance of softness to the physical realm around you to support your process.

It is also really important to have more conscious awareness of the moments we are in 5D perspective. Take note when the body feels different, when energy flows differently and when you are manifesting with ease. The more conscious we are, the more that can come in.

*See exercise WORKING WITH YOUR CHAKRAS AS THEY GO SPHERICAL in Healing Techniques and Exercises section connected to this aspect.

## SHIFT OF LOWER 4 BODIES TO UPPER 4 BODIES

The current human framework is predominantly focused on what can be termed the 'lower 4 bodies' which are the physical, mental, emotional and energy (auric) bodies. We all have an awareness of them and as we opened spiritually, the emotional and energy bodies were the primary focus or opening for higher vibrational energies to come in. They were also the primary focus of 'healing' and 'clearing' practices, such as shadow work, trauma release, auric field repair, and the like for decades. For years, releasing things was a long, sometimes arduous trek through the mud of our density that took weeks sometimes to release things, or deep dives into grief or depression to finally surface and find a lighter space. "How many layers does this onion have?", we asked ourselves each time we dove back into what felt like the same wounding, the same pattern.

When we did reach that lighter space and clarity came, we felt moments of bliss, transcendence, oneness. But, it was fleeting and hard to maintain. All of that work was needed to break the heavy patterns of the collective as well and it was done by the bold Indigos who came to break those walls down... to be the huge crashing wave that would hit the walls over and over until they crumbled. That gift has moved us into a period where things can be released almost instantly with the setting of intention and willingness to see Truth. And with the dawning of Truth, our mental bodies started being able to be 'broken open'. We can now see the glass cages of our belief structures that are literally the walls holding us in 3D.

As those walls get broken down, we come finally to the physical body; the lowest, slowest, densest of the four. It will be the most uncomfortable for us to move through, but will also reflect the clear progress directly for us. We will also begin to recognize how the 5 senses of our physicality that allow us to interact with it, actually anchor and hold us in 3D.

If we look at each of these, we have a clear comprehension of what lays ahead of us.

## Understanding the Transitions

**Energy body** - We start here by clearing debris and repairing auric field tears, etc

- This moves us towards the emotional body to release trauma (both energetic and emotional)

**Emotional body** - With the energy body really open, we can begin to release 'beliefs' connected to trauma

- Tapping into 'beliefs' moves that gaze towards the mental body to start to see limiting belief structures holding us back

**Mental body** - From recognizing belief structures, we can start to recognize mental structures connected to the 3D hologram

- From here, we can start to experience the hologram of the physical body

**Physical body** - This allows final release of physical 3D limitations and a movement into the full ability to hold the Solar Body in 'physicality.

One of the interesting pieces about the shifts in these 4 bodies is that as they lighten and heighten vibrationally, we remember and become aware of the rest of our bodies. We actually have what I have

termed the 'Fifth Dimensional Background Body' or 'Telepathic Communion Body' and the 'Sixth Dimensional Background Body' or 'Divine Communion Body'. The seventh is our actual full Solar Body (pka Light Body).

What will take place as we complete our ascension protocol is the merging of the 4 base level bodies (Physical, Mental, Emotional, Energy/Auric) into a singular platform that will then become the new 'physical body' (base layer) of our framework. The 5D telepathic body will correlate to the new mental structure, the 6D divine communion body to the new emotional structure and the solar/soul-ar body to the new energy body.

| Currently using | Upgrading to | Operates as |
| --- | --- | --- |
| | Solar Body | (new Energy body) |
| | 6D Divine Communion body | (new Emotional body) |
| Energy body | 5D Telepathic body | (new Mental body) |
| Emotional body | Merge to become base | |
| Mental body | physical body of Solar / | |
| Physical body | Light Body | |

Already, those that are quite open with their 'clairs' (clairvoyance, claircognizance, clairaudience, clairsentience, clairailience and clairgustance) are noticing how those signals are both strengthening and interweaving. This is the opening and development (remembrance) of the telepathic field (our 5D telepathic body), which is like the root ball where the signals for the clairs initiate and separate because they have to densify (slow down) in order for us to perceive them from the perspective point we sit within in 3D. As we shift our perspective point vibrationally higher, we begin to receive more of the root ball signal which receives all incoming energy instantaneously. Without having to break it down or slow it down, we become the embodied masters we were meant to be in full communication and connection with everything around us. This is our blueprinted true 'mental' structure. In developing our telepathic field, we become less reliant on our physical senses to receive information about our environment. We can then move to letting go of them as anchors and tools and allow them to simply be for enjoyment if and when we choose to revel in our physicality.

As the wisdom and power centers move into a merge in the heart, we are also no longer limited to receive energy from the divine via the crown chakra (see explanations of the path into polarity and our separation from the Divine stream of energy from Mother/Father God in 'Understanding the Path In' Section). Thus, the 6D body opens fully and we are able to be in constant communion with our Creator again.

This is a shift into 'dominion'. No longer cut off, veiled, boxed in or separated as we have been in 3D, our expansion truly is about full freedom on all levels. The physical body moves into full freedom of movement; the mental body into full freedom of thought; the emotional body into full freedom to emote as and when things are felt; the energy body into full freedom to energetically expand in any direction; the 5th dimensional telepathic body into full freedom of direct and transparent communication; the 6th dimensional divine communion body into the full freedom of unconditionality and the solar body in to the full freedom to BE.

One cannot reach the full freedom to BE if there is *lack* of freedom in any of the other layers. This is an important factor in the full merge into Self. If any part of your bodies is not FREE, it inhibits the full merging and step through into higher dimensional planes. Equally, any unconscious limitation to true freedom and autonomy that we have will block or repel the embodiment of it.

A beautiful dragon once put it this way: "Freedom is marked by the collar at the midline. It is pretty hard to control a dog whose collar is around their middle rather than their neck. In this analogy, the collar at the neck is others' beliefs or structures that someone else created. When you move into the middle path, the state of union, you are moving the collar to the middle or better yet, taking it off completely."

That said, we do also have some mechanisms that help us strip the bodies down to the core once the majority of our release work is complete. When your bodies are ready for this process, it should occur naturally and you may experience it like being in a gyroscope with 7 layers of what could be perceived as half-arcs like a big, open centrifuge. Each layer is allowing each of the bodies to 'spin out' the residue. You may simply experience it as waves of lightness or moments of dizziness or feeling like you are spinning.

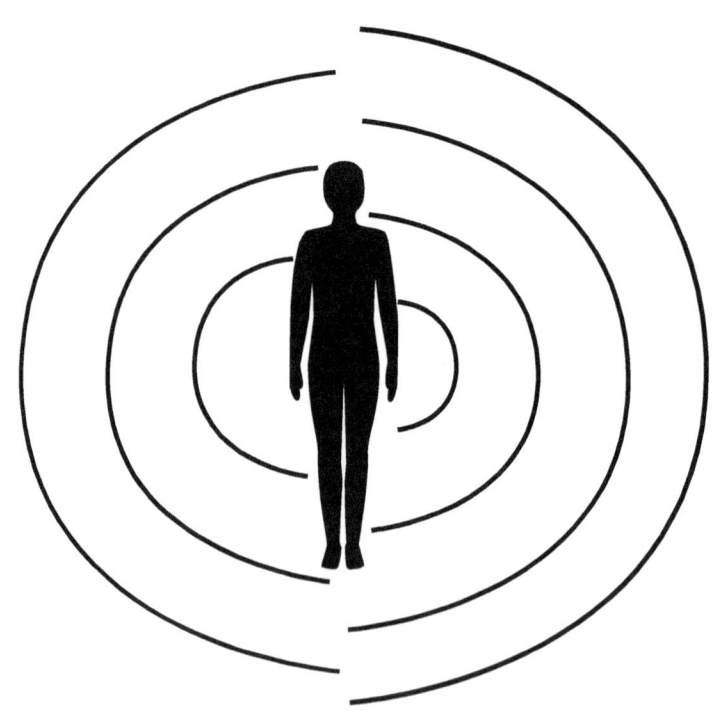

There are residual pieces as well, carried over from lifetimes that carry a charge. That charge may be coded with 'I can't' or 'I won't'. A charge of any kind can be pulled out once the major work is complete, because the completion of that work neutralizes or negates the other residue. Surrender to this process creates the 'slide' for things to fall away. Over and over again, the message from our higher Self is Surrender and Trust for the process to be able to complete.

## APPROACHING THE MENTAL AND PHYSICAL BODY SHIFTS

The first levels of merge with our Dragon or higher Self, whatever form your lineage may be, typically feels bodily as if you are taken into a bliss state… feeling light, giddy, tingly, expanded… but you can definitely feel the dragon format (or whatever your format is i.e. angelic, unicorn, etc.). You can feel the extensions or the edges of that and of yourself. It is important to reflect on that and be aware of it consciously, so that as you begin to move into a higher vibrational field within that merge you are able to really concretize consciously what the sensations and experiences are and how they differ. It is a marker of progression. It is also a preparation for your physical body to begin its subtle shifts.

As we have begun the move out of 3D and its polarized, densified vibration, our energy and emotional bodies have become more familiar with and accustomed to the field of potential, of Oneness. In this progression, many of the mental body structures that have limited us and boxed us in have also begun to fall away or be dissolved. It is the advancing proximity of the physical body to that field as we are in it more consistently that helps shift the physical tissues.

That field is where pure energy resides. Many experience it as pure silence, but a better word for it is 'reverence'. As you move into that field consciously, you will begin to experience it and your 'merged

state' differently, because your perspective point shifts. Rather than silence or emptiness, it becomes more like velvet with softness and depth to it. It's rich in texture. That texture permeates the field. It's not just something on the skin touching the skin. It's like the skin and everything internal turn into velvet and open up from silence into something with a pulse. This is where the true unity or merge state with your higher Self truly happens in order to exist within the 5D field as creator/manifestor living in alignment. As you touch that space, cognize it and make it bodily interpreted, it becomes your reality. This becomes the norm, this becomes what you go to naturally .

It's by those very subtle shifts in stages and making sure that you are notating and marking the differences that you keep moving into that deeper range of connection. This is what everyone will be doing. This is the process of moving deeper and deeper into that state of 'mersion' (a new word that has been coined by the Dragons). It's like merge and fusion together. When I first experienced 'mersion', it was as if the left and right hemispheres of my brain were coming together. I could feel the line of division between them around the center of the skull actually being diffused. It was a very new sensation. This is another aspect that we go through as we progress in what we keep calling ascension.

The sensations with this are like being fully encompassed by and expanded into the energy and yet simultaneously perfectly centered within yourSelf. The beautiful thing to note here is that the universal law of paradox becomes almost omnipresent with us as we move into a merged state. (see the section on Paradox)

That encompassing feeling for me is where I sense as if there's countless black tiles around me with space in-between them. It's all black, but I can perceive both the tiles and the space and it's in every direction around me; it's fully encompassing. That to me is encompassing. *And* at the same time in my heart space, if I was to go inward into my heart space, it's the same experience inwardly to a depth I can't even place. That's the centered feeling because it's such a big anchored space, like the center point of a black hole, that draws so much power within it. That's the field of reverence. It's the most centered and stable sensation that we can get to; really held in a pillar and yet expanded to such a degree and part of everything around you, that that sensation also exists of 'all encompassing'.

For those that struggle with being able to drop into that quiet, internal space or feel there's always clutter in the mind that wants to move through, gently remind yourself to drop deeper into the heart space. When you're in the heart space, the mind is far enough away that it's like a murmur outside on the street that you don't have to pay attention to and you'll get deeper and deeper in that heart space where it is pure reverence. There will be no sound, there will be no incoming signal other than pure heart communication.

This is how communication in the telepathic center feels. It is in the centerpoint of the heart, and it's like it rules out all other incoming sound, thought, distraction, disturbance… there's nothing but the incoming messages in that space. You remember how to be able to stay centered and focused in it in a way that it's all that exists. And yet, at the same time, there's some external awareness that you are in the field as your human self and that you're receiving it and understanding it.

It is only in your heart where you can get into that state of reverence where all knowing exists. There's a term for all knowing - omniscient - in our vocabulary for a reason; because beings have reached that state of 'mersion' where they do know everything that their soul level knows. There's been a misguided interpretation of its meaning that an omniscient Being knows everything that God knows. Truly the word omniscient can be applied the way we always apply it to God as a creative source, that field of energy is indeed omniscient. But, when we apply it to ourselves, we can only be omniscient of that which we have experienced and learned on soul level, or can absorb from being connected into that state.

On a soul level, where we are created, where we are brought through and created as a soul in the many, many realms that exist, God creates our consciousness with the capacity, the field of potential to absorb all that God knows, all that God is. But, we start in a field or realm that has limitations, because every experiment that God creates is about a different set of parameters and whether those parameters can actually reach completion. Can they actually absorb and come back fully into all that they know is God and become that?

So each of those individual creations is omniscient within its capacity of what it knows, but until one reaches the full knowing of God, there's always more to learn and more to experience. This is why we continue to have incarnations in so many different places and are continually expanding. This is what the term old soul that is often used means. It is one that has had the opportunity for more learning, more experiences, and more collection of knowing, information and experience held within their signature. So they are an expanded field of energy with a more complex soul signature.

You recognize them walking down the street or in a group of people because when you meet them and feel their energy, you're picking up on the complexity within their soul signature that has had so many things added to it because of all of their incarnational learning. They're just at a different level of experience than what might be called 'younger' or less experienced souls. Because we are in a time-space continuum, the appropriate word is an old soul. They've been around a long time from this perspective. The complexity of their energetic signature reveals that they are a master. They are what might be considered a higher level of mastery versus being 'old' as a soul. Even that subtle distinction, in your brain pattern, in your brain waves, helps you move towards the field where our guides and higher Self sit.

If those are the terms we use in communication that are more true, that hold more truth within them in a unified field, when we begin to use those terms, we move into coherence with that field. You begin to move away from where you might describe something as old and the timeline constraint that that puts on it. It is another step of moving you out of that time-space continuum dependence.

Have you considered that we are in a state of co-dependence with the time-space continuum? We have not wanted to look at it as something we're dependent upon, but rather that we're stuck in. There's another subtle vocabulary shift to help the mental body release its anchors in 3D: that we are stuck in, anchored in, held in, a time space continuum that we're trying to break free of or move out of. When we very subtly shift our brain wave to say, 'well, actually, I'm dependent on this time-space continuum,' it shifts the responsibility to us in our choicepoints.

Just like a co-dependent relationship, one stays in the relationship for what their getting out of it. That is a powerful statement. We are staying dependent on it, because we're getting something out of it. When we can answer the question of what it is that we are getting out of the time-space continuum, we'll break another link in our dependence on it. When those subtle truths hit our mental bodies, you can feel spaces in the brain that open like flowers, almost like there's electrical energy or a molten field bubbling up and opening in the brain. That's the power of language. It's the power of words. Language holds spells within it that anchor us in physicality.

We are literally in the process of changing the 'language of our reality'. We are deconstructing reality as we have believed it to operate and have operated within it. As we drop each definition, we get to play in a bigger field that has deeper meaning and is an unfolding, constant greater awareness of something bigger. Once you start learning to drop the definitions, it becomes easier and easier, like learning a new language. Once you learn the basics and conjugation, you learn new vocabulary faster and easier. You become fluent.

When you're stuck, you're a victim. When we shift the words of being stuck in something to being dependent on something, it becomes a self-responsible choice that you've made to stay in it, and it allows you to move that one step further. It's sort of like an alcoholic who can't even see it. One day they wake up and they can say 'I'm an alcoholic', and that's when the change can start taking place. When you realize you're dependent on the time-space continuum by choice, it will empower you to move into recognizing what you're getting out of that dependence. Then, you will move to a state where you realize that you don't need or desire that, and you'll feel those tethers popping off or falling away. Your experiences will get less and less constrained by the field of the time-space continuum around you, because that's all it is quite literally.

Our 'created' reality structure is someone else's construct that we have bought into. Ten people each have their own perception of reality. They might all agree on a 'color', but in Truth they might all be seeing it differently. When we realize this, we can step into our mastery where we each get to choose our own reality. You might keep certain constructs in common, like 'the sky is blue', but in Truth we will eventually come to realize that we can choose to see it as purple or red if we choose. It is ok to choose to align to the trees being 'green' as long as we allow them to be more than that if they are.

If you could see it from where your Soul level sits, it is like a bubble of constraint. For those that feel stuck in it, it is like a quagmire. It is simply a bubble of constraint that all of humanity is within. In 3D, there is an x-y axis configuration where one axis is time, the other is space. In universal Truth, there's all kinds of other vectors and axes. Where we sit, our reality is the very tiniest point of intersection on that entire grid. That point is the land of form while the expansion of dimensions exists in all other directions from that point. When we're no longer constrained or dependent on that field, we can move into a totally different relationship with both time and space.

If we are at the intersection point, then we have the capacity to move out of that and move up or down the time continuum. We actually do that when we explore past and future lives. We can also move along the space continuum, in and out of dimensional pockets, You do this in meditation consciously as you move into different experiences. What we haven't yet realized is all of the other axes or vectors that we can explore beyond those constraints, that are also part of the field. We don't yet really have terminology or words in our languaging that would help us grasp them. They become experiential as you move into compliance with them.

So ask in the heart, what do I get out of being dependent on the time space-continuum? One of the biggest things that comes for humans is stability. The time-space continuum from where we sit is the most stable thing in our field. Because of our physicality, we need to feel an alignment to our gravitational field or something that stabilizes our molecular structure. That's the greatest thing that we're dependent upon, based on our field of experience. But we can shift that and will need to in order to move into full ascension while maintaining 'physicality'. Think of the experience that Christ showed us while on the planet. The expression of his body after he rose and left his physical body behind was a pure light structure and yet he was still recognized. He was still able to take the form of what his body had looked like when he walked in a physical body. This is the power of the shift into your body of light, your solar body.

That concept isn't quite being embraced by the mental body fully yet as to how our body would incorporate light to such a degree to be walking like Yeshua did after his ascension, after he rose and walked out of the tomb. The hard part is that we don't have the parameter of being able to do that but keep our physical cells. So how does that light structure emanate through physicality to make me feel stabilized in a different way than I feel stabilized in the time-space continuum? In Yeshua's example, because of that emanation of light, he was not constrained by physicality. He walked through the rock wall. So he cannot be constrained. He cannot be dependent on the time-space continuum because he walked right through space. He walked right through the spaces in-between of those rocks.

So how do we do that coming from our physicality, in full trust and surrender to our higher knowing? You have to keep surrendering your trust into it. The bridge is there in the movement into the heart into the space of reverence. This brings our emotional and energy bodies that much deeper into it, which forces the mental and physical bodies to follow because they cannot be what we might call stretched out or too far away from each other. They have to stay in a proximal energetic relationship. And so, as you bring yourself fully into that heart space, into that state of reverence, into that unique conscious place, you will begin to shift. This is where the triggers get flipped because of the physical body desiring to follow suit. In order to follow along towards that vibrational energetic component shift, it will have the inner knowing whether it's conscious or not, of what the cells need to do to move out of dependence on the time-space continuum, and thus shift their molecular structure that very subtle bit that then pushes them to shift from carbon to silica. This allows the transformation into emanating light in a stabilized way such that you no longer need carbon and matter to be stabilized within.

So there are critical keys sitting within this sphere of reverence. This is the state we want to keep returning to. This is what will allow the mental body to trust and surrender and continue to expand in vibration. Part of the challenge of moving away from dependence on the time-space continuum is that the mental body feels safe and comfortable because the physical body is stabilized. As we move towards destabilizing, that makes the mental body uncomfortable. When it has the information, then it can surrender and relax into it. So each step along this path, each of these gentle pushes forward are bringing us to that space.

It all hinges on this concept of being dependent on the time-space continuum. That is huge. It is like putting the whole ascension process in a single statement of contemplation. That's going to be what takes us miles further on the next part of the journey.

## SHIFTING THE MENTAL BODY

**Exercises to break belief structures/mental body limits.**

The mental body truly wants to cling to 'reality' as it has known it to be. It is a very uncomfortable process to let go of the structures that you have accepted as 'real' and yet are now realizing hold so much more. To be asked to allow this reality to be perceived as the hologram that it is, which is basically a projection of light particles, is REALLY hard for the brain. But when we allow these concepts to ease in gently, we allow that shift to begin. Our task is to drop the definitions within your mental body that hold your current perception of 'reality' in place and open it to its full potential and greater or no definition at all. You could almost consider your conceptual definition of reality to be the final frontier as you move into a new reality.

As your higher consciousness merges into your mental body, you begin to have a different sensation in understanding or grasping things. You start to have more *'aha'* moments that incorporate deep knowing through the body as a whole. What is unfolding is your brain coming back online to its full capacity rather than being limited to its less than 5% usage here in 3D. Consciousness and higher Truth coming in/being remembered increases electrical, magnetic and energetic connectivity within the brain. You are literally lighting it up! This also creates new neural pathways and meridians, which can make it hard to focus. Many experience this as 'fog brain'.

A key here is "conceptual awareness" or "perceptive awareness". We know that both 3D and 5D exist on both sides of the zero-point doorway. When we allow the implosion or inversion through the centerpoint and the expansion of awareness from there, we have to both

be ready for and allow the new perceptive experience. We have to find and allow the spaces in-between of the structural reality of 3D around us to open up just like we did when we first started merging with our higher energy body. This allows the field of potential to expand around us and pull us up and out of the fixed 3D pattern.

Imagine a ride on a roller coaster. You ride it over and over and are quite comfortable with it, know what to expect, when you will get off, etc. Well, at the end of the ride, you come into the station and realize the cars can go onto a bigger roller coaster around the one you have been on. Once you leave the station, you lose awareness of the first, smaller roller coaster, even though it is still there. Where do you want your perceptive awareness to be? On the smaller roller coaster (3D) or the larger (5D and beyond)? You do have the ability to choose in every moment!

## WHAT YOU BELIEVE IS WHAT YOU CREATE, WHAT YOU CREATE IS WHAT YOU BECOME

These exercises allow us to break through the Matrix/Reality/Hologram structure we have been perceiving.

**Perceiving the inversion exercise:**

The idea is to allow yourself to see the light structure of things around you or their sacred geometric structure that all things in 3D have as an underlying template in the 5th dimension.

Start with a piece of fruit such as a grape or a peach.

Allow yourself to let the physicality of the grape fall away as you let the light field or sacred geometry, the grape's signature structure, to be perceived. It is sort of like allowing yourself to see the energy/auric field of a tree or person, but opens it up to all energies around you, whether they hold consciousness or not, and is about seeing their inversion rather than their energy body; like seeing a city skyline silhouette, but instead of dark buildings against a sunset sky, the buildings are pure Light and geometry. This is what the true structure looks like beyond 3D.

**Seeing through the spaces in-between:**

The idea is to allow yourself to see what is beyond a 'physical' object.

There are two ways to work with this one.

One: Have someone put an object (organic energy items like fruit that have life force are easier to start with) behind a bowl or something larger than it without letting you know what that object is. Your task is to allow yourself to see beyond and 'through' the bowl as if looking through its spaces in-between in order to perceive what is beyond it. By focusing on the energy signature of the objects beyond it, you exercise your own capacity to recognize energy and allow the telepathic body to open its receptors.

Two: Sit where there are 2 windows opening onto a view that have a wall or walls between them, ideally of trees or a building or something that extends into view in both. Your task is to allow yourself to see beyond the 'walls' in between the windows and pick up the details of what that tree or building 'looks' like if the walls weren't there. Again, you are letting the energetic signature of it fill you in on its blueprint structure and information without relying on the eyes.

Of note in both of these is also the fact that you are allowing your mental body to open up to the reality of underlying energetic signature and structure within all of reality around you. Eventually, you may perceive more light, color and geometry within all the trees in your neighborhood, for example, than you see of their bark, branches and leaves.

**Tiling of dimensions:**

This analogy allows the mind to open up to higher Truth to understand or conceptualize moving into higher dimensional spaces and 'unity' consciousness.

Imagine that our energy signature is made up of a series of binary code - 1s and 0s - that are represented by tiles. These are all the unique vibrational pulses that define us. As they slow in vibration (densify), they are perceived as a descriptive hologram with depth in 3D. The tiles meet and create a picture that is 'who we are'. The tiles could actually densify all the way down to 2D, but that is too slow for consciousness to be held or maintained. It would look like vinyl flooring. In 3D, the layers and layers of tiles give it 'depth' because they offset from each other within the vibrational wave where they sit. In 4D, an 'outward' offset is added, while in 5D an 'inward' offset is added.

In 'unity' consciousness, we perceive being 'one' with all first because we have a divine connection point in common in the Soul Seed, but second because in higher vibrational sequencing, the expanded offset of the tile configuration allows all of the signals or 'signatures' to interweave in and through each other with matching waves intertwining. If you can imagine two Beings or objects side-by-side whose tiles are expanding outward (and inward - that one is hard for the brain) from the accustomed 3D placement and the spaces-in-between stretching and revealing, you will be able to envision this interweaving of the tiles.

From our 3D mental body perspective, this expansion is a deep penetration into a huge unknown. It requires a deep trust in Self to keep going. That is one thing that has been a consistent part of my own expansion over the last 7 years: deeper and deeper levels of trust. How much can I trust mySelf as the one leading me forward into all of these unknown realms, consistently breaking new barriers of what I have known before? I realized that our mental bodies even have a subtle boundary for what we know as 'infinity'. Boundaries make us feel safe and comfortable, but this journey is about moving beyond all of them. You have to see the edges of 3D to move beyond it.

We come to recognize that *everything* is energy; vibrational waves made up of strings of code (the tiles or characteristics of that field). Where they meet is what gives you a 3D, 4D, 5D or beyond experience. 3D is just slowed down enough to see them as matter with our 'senses'. When they speed up, they are more like the surface of the ocean which is hard to 'stabilize' for perception with anything other than our telepathic field or energy body. This is why 'destabilizing' our field of reality is the perfect terminology for our mental body to grasp our movement into that ocean. We have always been part of it, but our perspective point has resided in the lower density of its perception, thus we perceived 'matter'. Our next level as we shift the perspective point is to become part of that ocean; no longer even just seeing it or knowing it is there, but actually becoming part of it and letting go of what we used to 'see'. We have to stretch past our comfort zones and boundaries, particularly our reliance on our 3D senses to get there.

**Contemplation:**

It only exists if you believe it exists. Let that sink in.

**Stepping into unity ('mersion'):**

This allows us to dissolve the barrier between the two hemispheres of the brain that up until now have needed to be polarized fields with different functions. As ascension progresses, we will feel these merge or fuse energetically, which is the concept of this new term 'mersion'. This moves us toward the ability to see all potential outcomes of each choicepoint and consciously choose the highest path forward, rather than relying solely on learning from past choices or information. In connection with the telepathic field, so much more information

becomes available and our heart's desire is to choose the highest or most loving path at each choicepoint.

Mersion will be a natural process that unfolds as you move deeper and deeper into the merge within yourself and with your full Self. Knowing that it is a part of the process will help you recognize what is happening when the sensations in the brain and mental body begin.

As you can see, the mental body will go through some tremendous shifts in order to up-level its perception. The mental and physical bodies are definitely the hardest and most uncomfortable for us. What if someone were to say to you '"Reality" is a blank slate in every moment'. Can you actually align to that Truth and allow it to be? Most likely, there are a myriad of oppositions already rising from the mental body… but… but… but.

It is through the release of all that we want to cling to of our knowing and understanding of this reality that we will return to mastery and be free. When in our mastery, we create from the True desires of our hearts and intentions in every moment in full alignment to ourSelves. This is how the journey of life becomes/is magic. The beauty of this experiment is that for the first time on this planet, we will reach the capacity to live that embodiment while maintaining a physical expression. So now we approach the physical shifts that will allow our full Divine Human Blueprint to be realized.

## SHIFT FROM CARBON TO SILICA

We have briefly discussed the zero-point gateway. We literally go through an inversion as we move through it and come to realize that reality as we have experienced it has actually been inside out and upside down. The principle of enfoldment in action. In one sense, we could say that as we 'invert' or 'right ourselves' we become the shadow of what we knew ourselves to be. The other side of that gateway has always been experienced as something outside of ourselves as we have touched it with our emotional or energy bodies. It felt like the 'void of creation': that empty blackness pulsing with life. It is on the other side of this gateway as we bring our physical body through and into full alignment with that universal pulse that we biologically shift from carbon to silica. When that occurs, pin points of light can then start to refract through the silica structure and emit light. Our Solar Body can come through and shine fully! The structure of silica itself lends to light refraction because it is both more spacious and more geometrically faceted than carbon.

This will be an unfolding process. As we release densities in our field and incorporate more Light, we begin the activation of our crystalline aspect. As discussed in 'Our Path In', it was the crystal stream of energy that split into the black and white streams in the creation of a polarized field. As part of that densification, there were genetic manipulations done to humanity that resulted in dormant, mis-aligned and mis-paired DNA strands within our field. These are what have kept us in the dark. Just prior to or as part of our crystalline DNA aspect activating, we will experience the coming online of these. This DNA activation is like strewn confetti being reversed in time to a hover state in mid-air where the electro-magnetic pull can draw pairs together and re-sequence them properly. This facilitates the returning to the crystalline stream in which our full crystalline DNA is activated and our full Divine Human Blueprint is accessible.

One of the first things that happens is the 'popping' of our DNA 'double helix' structure, which is aligned to polarity, into its full trinary helix. This activation is assisted by the White and Crystal Dragons.

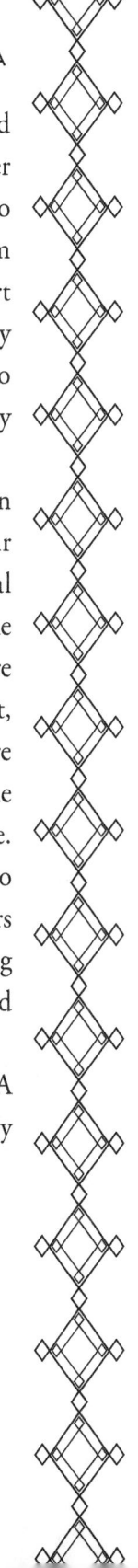

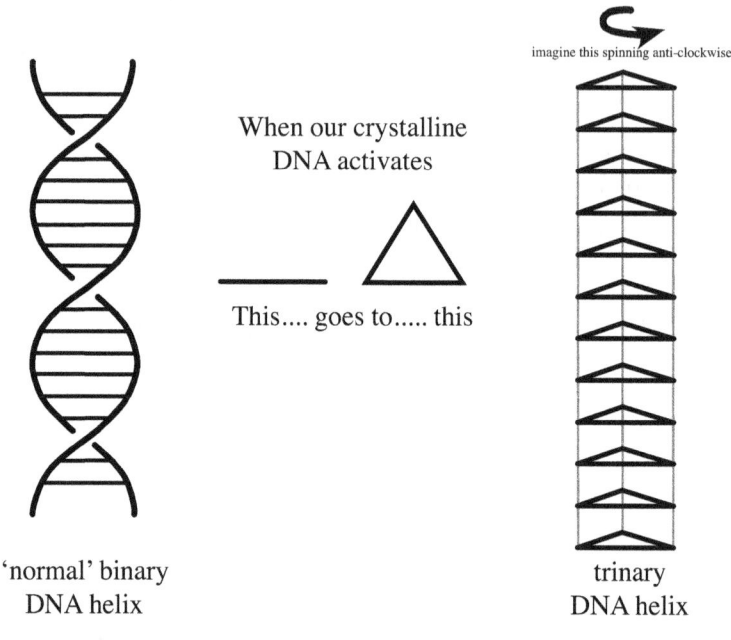

imagine this spinning anti-clockwise

When our crystalline
DNA activates

This.... goes to..... this

'normal' binary
DNA helix

trinary
DNA helix

When this begins, it is usually simultaneous with or spurs the beginning of the activation of our crystalline geometries. We each have 77 crystalline geometries: 11 distinct crystalline structures associated with each of the 7 core human chakras. Each of the 11 'layers' is associated with the dimensional layers of this universe from 2D to 12D. You don't have to consciously know what they are, but you will have a sense of how many of them are activated as you progress. The core and first geometry that activates is your central pillar that runs like a crystal wand between the Power Center (center of the Womb/ Hara space also known as the Dantian), the Heart and the Wisdom Center (center of the amygdala and pineal gland structures at the tip of the brain stem). When we have this aligned, there is pure White Divine Light flowing through the Wisdom Center; the pineal gland is open and flowing with 'pure knowing'. There is also pure Divine Black Light flowing in the Dantian and we are open and flowing with 'pure creation' energy. Our ability to manifest and create becomes almost instantaneous. This is due to the incredible clarity and strength of the electro-magnetic field we are outputting at this point.

The next progression will be the shift of the trinary helix into a diamond helix structure. This occurs as the amount of Light moving up the central pillar (your core crystalline geometry) continues to increase. Some of the increase in light is due to your own releases, deep work and intention. There is also a great deal coming in from the increased solar flare activity which is pure Divine Light being made available to assist humanity.

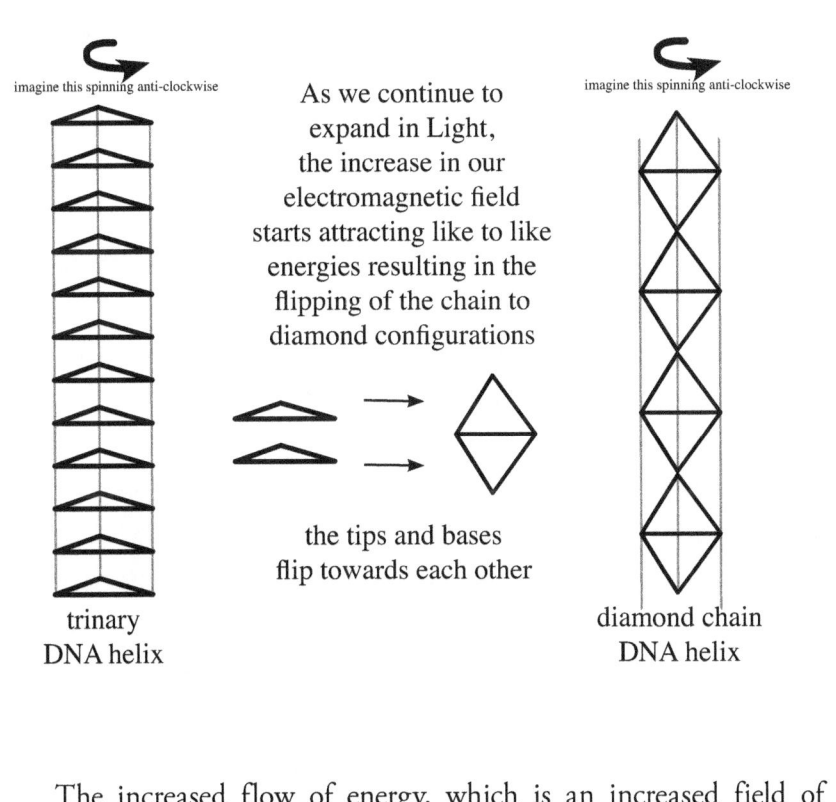

imagine this spinning anti-clockwise

As we continue to expand in Light, the increase in our electromagnetic field starts attracting like to like energies resulting in the flipping of the chain to diamond configurations

the tips and bases flip towards each other

imagine this spinning anti-clockwise

trinary
DNA helix

diamond chain
DNA helix

The increased flow of energy, which is an increased field of electromagnetism, up the central channel of the DNA trinary helix begins to align like energies to like energies resulting in the flipping of the chain to diamond configurations with every other trine flipping its

magnetic alignment so that bases and tips begin to meet. There is also a movement starting towards multidirectionality/multidimensionality as we merge more and more directly with our solar body. Like all else in the journey, movement of energy will no longer be linear. Any of these stages can be experienced as electrical jolts as energy moves into and up the spine with more intensity.

The diamond-shaped merkabah that we have had access to while here in the Earth plane has been directly associated with the limited path of energy we can access here. Our heart or soul seed point lies at the center, but that energy has been pulled up to an apex aligned to white (Light) energy, down to an apex aligned to black (Shadow) energy and from there out to 4 corners points that are the elementals of our 3D field (Earth, Air, Fire and Water).

Moving back into alignment with our higher crystalline capacity and deeper merge with the full solar body, centralizes that energy again and brings the merkabah into a spinning, spiraling holographic diamond chain. This creates spin in both directions along the channel as our energy is ascending (anti-clockwise spin) while our solar body energy is descending (clockwise spin) to merge with us. It doesn't spin only one way or the other. It is "in motion", meaning both directions (or actually all directions when we can conceptualize that) weave through each other in balance. "In motion" is a non-directional term. Directions are inherently part of 'duality' and 'linear' realities. It becomes a diamond chain and takes our 'merkabah' to the next level.

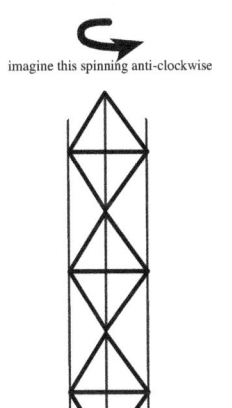

imagine this spinning anti-clockwise

imagine this spinning in all directions
inwardly and outwardly

As we merge with our solar
body soul level diamond
helix that rises from within,
it moves us into the full
holographic diamond
configuration

The holographic merkabah is
"in motion"
(all directions weave through
each other in perfect balance)

diamond chain
DNA helix

double diamond
DNA helix

You may experience the
double diamond helix
as something like this in meditations

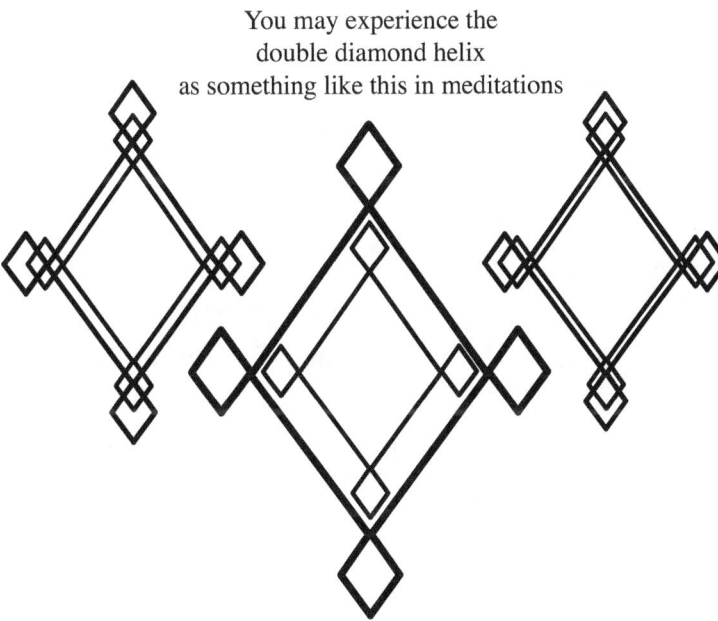

As the electrical energy within the diamond chain increases, we begin to feel 'sparks' or 'electrical pops' in our field, particularly in the physical body. We are beginning the transition from molecular elemental bonding to what the Dragons have called 'etheric bonding', which is a geometric structure of Light rather than actual merged elements like $H_2O$. The water in our bodies is what begins to carry more Light and thus shift first. It begins to conduct more and more electromagnetic energy through the body tissues and allows the predominant carbon structures to 'pop' into a silica structure, which is a very subtle geometric shift, but allows the higher etheric structure to hold a great deal more light.

The amount of crystalline light in our field is what allows the metamorphosis of the elemental bonding to shift to etheric bonding. This is what 'holding your light' or 'Being the Light' actually means. It is quite literal. Remember, we are in an inverted reality, so looking at this in a subtly different way might help it click. What does it take to make a diamond in 3D. Heat and pressure. Invert that. What does it take to move into etheric diamond... light and expansion. The higher the vibration of your signal, the more space in between, the more light can radiate. That first moment of shift is the shift point synthesis and is exactly like the first moment that coal begins to turn into diamond.

What is unique and inherent within your own diamond structure is that at the centerpoint of each 'diamond' is your geometric soul signature lit up within a spinning Metatron's Cube (that is universal). This is you aligning to your full Soul structure, which is why 'pure knowing' comes in as a state of Being. All that you know at Soul level becomes accessible again. It is also an inherent part of aligning to any dimensional field above 3D. We have to be in our own diamond structure in our field to not be collapsed by the Quantum Field or misaligned within it. If you are familiar with the Philadelphia Experiment in 1943, it was an attempt to teleport a U.S. Navy destroyer from Philadelphia, Pennsylvania to Norfolk, Virginia. It resulted in many men dying because they were stuck in the hull structure of the ship as it was brought back through the quantum field.

A natural part of our expansion will be the movement into multidimensional consciousness. Up until now, only our energy and emotional bodies have not been limited by the space continuum aspect of 3D. If you have experienced the time continuum warping and operating strangely, you will be able to recognize the space continuum beginning to do so as your field of matter shifts. The light codes expanding within you trigger your physical body to expand into the spaciousness around you beginning up to about 12 inches around you. Thus far, we have been anchored into singularity consciousness because of our alignment within the vectors of the time-space continuum. But, as we unlock that anchor, we allow a greater interface with all systems and open to full multidimensional consciousness. Becoming functionally present in multiple 'places' at once is true multi-tasking.

This raises an interesting aspect connected to our ability to teleport. Once we have full multidirectionality and multidimensionality capacity, I believe we will remember how to do so. It is wholly dependent on a silica state in our cells and the ability to align each cell into a unified intention to the pulse signature of our destination. (Please see the section on Teleportation)

Exercise: Move into a quiet meditation with the intention of connecting to your crystalline DNA and Solar Body structure. Ask 'what is stuck in my lower body DNA as contract or karma? Where can light not penetrate because of a false belief structure? And let yourself receive the information. Often just bringing it into consciousness is all that is needed to shift it.

Knowledge of 'karmic knots' may be helpful here. Karmic knots are leftover densities literally on the spine or central pillar that look or feel like a cluster of dense matter. They are residual karmic unresolved or unreleased debt carried often over lifetimes surrounding the same

lesson. If you are shown any of these, ask your guides what needs to be done to release them. The Black Dragon is a great ally for this work.

## OCULAR NERVE SHIFTS AND THE SENSES GOING SPHERICAL

The optic nerve, much like the brain has not been able to operate at its full capacity within this realm. It's severing was part of the DNA manipulation of humanity as it dropped in density. It actually has the ability to see holographically. It isn't just about external *or* internal vision. The activation of it, which involves re-pairing of the DNA to align with our blueprint, works to expand internal and external vision and merge them. That allows us to 'see' the fabric of reality as it truly is - the overlays (multidimensional layers), the matrix, the geometric fields of Beings around us, etc. The rods and cones in use within duality operate purely as binary code, but when we expand our DNA to its crystalline aspect and the full trinary helix, it can begin to operate holographically.

This idea could be expanded to encompass all of our senses. Not only do our chakras shift from linear to spherical, but as we progress we start to recognize and allow our senses to do the same. Our five physical senses are actually one of our biggest anchors to 3D and thus one of our biggest hurdles to move out of 3D perspective. We are comfortable having sound come in through a linear channel into the inner ear to be perceived and translated. We are comfortable having sensation hit the skin and be both detected and defined. We are comfortable having taste or smell sensations come in linearly to the taste buds and nostrils. What does it even mean to allow those to be perceived and experienced spherically?

It means that we don't limit the signal to those receptors. We allow those to be *part* of the perception. We let the energy signal of that sound, smell, taste or touch to also be perceived with the telepathic body. This allows seeing, tasting, touching, hearing, and smelling to have both its inward and outward component simultaneously without needing it to be focused on a single point of 'contact'. It allows the telepathic body to come fully online and our interaction with our environment or reality to be much more rich by receiving its full signal. Colors, sounds, and sensations all become more vibrant and alive. The world becomes more magical to move through and we become more directly interconnected with it by experiencing its fullness rather than a single channel of its output.

The opening of the telepathic body is a key element in our movement into the communal harmonic field of the 5D New Earth. We become able to read and send information/energy instantaneously. What does this actually look like in action? Picture a large, crowded space such as a train station. You need to move from one side to the other quickly and easily. When your heart starts holding that intention, all others who also have their telepathic field open and are part of the communal harmonic pick up on it instantly. They begin to move aside to honor that desire and a path opens for you. This is happening for all present and where they need to go or whether they are staying stationary. The ease of flow through the space is harmonious for all.

## OTHER BODY CHANGES

One of the very interesting things I perceive shifting as we merge completely with our Solar Bodies is our eye color. For years, Tiamat, who is the Mother of Chaos Dragon and acted as Gaia's guardian, always presented to me with brilliant, glowing red eyes. It was a fierce energy presentation as part of her test of humans. She was always peering at me through portals from where she was holding Gaia into our 3D field. Back in 2020, during one of our meditations and work with the construction of the golden scaffolding within the new Earth template, she came forward and was looking at me with clear, golden

eyes. They were so soft, loving and beautiful. I realized that we were meeting in a pure 5D space and that in this field, where the energy had not slowed or densified so greatly, the true vibration/color of her eyes could be perceived.

I believe ours will be the same. I have witnessed my own eyes slowly shifting as I evolve. I have always had a thin band of translucent color around the outside edge of the iris, which is green, but can appear blue depending on what I wear. What I find fascinating is that the translucent aspect of this ring is widening and I get the sense that when we have fully shifted, our eyes will be translucent rather than opaque. Our eyes will literally be letting more Light shine through. I believe dark eyes (brown and black) will go to grey or silver, while lighter opaque blue and green shades will become translucent blue and green.

We will not need food.
We will not need water.
We will not need to breathe.

How crazy does it sound to read those facts? Your divine human blueprint body is designed to be totally self sufficient from external dependence. Much like plants, we have within our design the ability to photosynthesize sunlight for energy, which eliminates the need for food, water and air. This is why the correction was made to my label of 'Light Body' that was a good term for many years, but needed to evolve closer to Truth. We are Solar Beings, created in divine alignment with the source energy that births and emanates through solar bodies, particularly those that are considered 'suns' (central suns, great central suns, greater central suns, etc.) They are all in pure connection with and emanating the divine light of Mother/Father God as do we. When we 'micro' this information into our own template, we are like our own sun and solar system, as is each cell in our body. Just allow that to sink in and percolate for a while.

What we find as we begin to vibrate higher (faster) and hold more Light, our body begins to naturally desire 'lighter' food. Our experience of foods will shift with us, particularly as we begin to see the inversion or energy form of the food we are ingesting. In 3D, just like the loss of electrical current across really long extension cords, our own bodies light waves were densified enough that we needed another energy source (food) because our own light coming in through layers of density met enough resistance and lost enough force that we needed an external 'plug in' for energy. In 5D, the 'food' may still be there until we can fully process light, but it will not be in our experience as slow and dense as 'matter' that we have known. It will become more of an experience of an energy 'form'. An important note here is that our physical bodies as they shift physiologically and biologically may experience a level of depletion, particularly of Vitamins A, C, D and K. It is recommended to ingest more *orange* foods, particularly the skin and rind to support the body when this arises.

## The shift of the breath/lungs expanding to operate within 5D:

One of the things that will change greatly as we move into alignment with our full Solar bodies is our need to breathe with the lungs. At some point, much like you may have experienced in a deep meditative or samadhic state, you will come to notice that your breath can come in or out through all of the spaces in-between of the organs, skin and tissues It is the activation of the High Heart chakra and the Sun (or High Solar Plexus) chakra that allow the lungs and organs to expand into the spaces in-between.

This then leads to the transition of the organs to move away from 'food' dependence and towards nourishment from Light. This is part of the reason to practice the exercise of seeing the inversion with fruit. We begin to recognize the life force as being the 'true nourishment' rather

than the flesh or matter of the fruit. Hand in hand with this shift is the increase of solar energy via flares being sent and received by the body that charges the electrical field to make the carbon to silica shift. This increase also directly affects the organs as it helps move the toxin load out of our cells, particularly the stored toxicity in the liver and kidneys. All organ cleanses at this point will support the process and many often note headaches as a common part of the process because of both the increased electrical energy and the toxin load release.

Another common symptom is feeling exhausted. Indeed, we are literally expelling the exhaust or toxins from the body as we up-level. Allowing the body to rest when it needs to is not only key for this aspect, but as practice in honoring the flow of our own knowing. Every time we override it with 'have to', 'should' or 'need to', we take a couple of steps backwards.

As we move into the ascension process, it is also a strong probability that a grieving process starts. This seems counter-intuitive as it is what we have been seeking and longing for. Indeed, it is one of the paradoxes we experience because we have the ecstatic experiences of magic and alignment unfolding in our journey. But, at the same time part of us moves into grieving the loss of things on Earth as we have known them to be. This may include the loss of a lot of relationships that can't move forward because they are no longer in alignment vibrationally or able to exist within the same vibrational parameters.

## CONNECTING TO THE FULLNESS OF OUR SOUL SELF

Obviously there is quite a set of shifts taking place during this process. Much of it can be disconcerting, overwhelming and oddly isolating even though we are moving into a harmonic of unity consciousness. It is important and helpful to continually be bold enough to have conversations with others you sense are on the same path. If nothing else, it will give you the confidence to keep going and confirm that you are definitely not crazy and not alone.

As if all the changes we will experience in this earthly form weren't enough to take in, there is one more aspect to discuss. That is what happens as we fully start to connect to our Solar Body. Moving into full connection isn't just a connection with yourSelf at Soul level. It is also the reconnection with every other aspect of yourSelf that is currently incarnate in all realms.

That can entail information about 'past' lives in this Earth plane (I put that in quotes because they are actually concurrent when outside the time-space framework). It can also be glimpses and 'memory' of incarnations happening within other star systems in this universe. What I have found is that the further forward I go on my journey, the further back I can remember. The pieces and bread crumbs start popping in along with the information they hold. It may still feel like a huge puzzle being assembled very haphazardly, but be assured it is coming together.

Some of the most useful analogies for the ascension process are often using language associated with computer systems. In this instance, you can imagine your entire super computer (Soul) that has mainframes in multiple buildings and they have not been connected yet. Or more accurately, all the others have been connected, but your building has been offline. Essentially, we are plugging in those connections so the entire IT system is operational and conscious. That brings about awareness within each mainframe of all of the other mainframes and all of the other buildings.

I bring this up because it can be disconcerting to start having conscious recall of events happening in your other 'bodies'. Many of my clients describe feeling like timelines are collapsing or being able to see more than one timeline or dimension simultaneously or as if their awareness is blinking back and forth between the two. Indeed, our process is actively cohesing the dimensional overlays together.

## THE ASCENSION PROTOCOL

I had a powerful experience in the summer of 2023 when backpacking in the Yosemite wilderness. I was high on a ridge staring out at a wilderness that had no visible end. In that instant, I felt this powerful knowing land within my body that there were at least 5 other aspects of myself experiencing the same thing at the same moment but in other worlds. Staring into a vast wilderness, all very different of course, but simultaneously aligned. That was just a momentary glimpse, but that experience is one of the steps towards that becoming the constant moment-to-moment norm that lies ahead on the journey. Quantum baby steps.

Another huge alignment when merging into our Soul level Self is reawakening our true heart desires and the ability to be in 'flow' with those. Stress, worry, anxiety, struggle with decisions... they literally cease to exist as you move into your greatest level of Trust with your Self. Most of us lost the ability to be in alignment with our true heart desires at a very young age. I would actually bet that if you asked most adults out there what their heart truly desired, they would struggle to answer because we are so disconnected from our True Heart that we wouldn't even know. And if they could answer, they wouldn't believe it really possible to have or do whatever it is. They would default to what their day planner calendar shows them is next.

There are a myriad of reasons we might come up with to stick to the planner. Nearly all of them are external constructs. To be respectable, to be respectful, to be responsible, to be trustworthy... none of them matter if you can't be in true joy from the heart in what you are doing.

Our natural state is actually JOY. Hard to believe isn't it? I wouldn't say that I have felt a lot of joy in my life, particularly as an adult with the weight of responsibilities constantly present. Momentary joys and highs, but definitely not a prolonged state. I am not talking hear about happiness, contentment or peace either. I am talking about pure, ecstatic, overflowing and ebullient JOY.

How can we actually be aligned to the joy of our Soul when we can't even hear what our Heart desires? We can't. And that is why as we come closer and closer to knowing the Truth of ourselves by releasing trauma, breaking down belief structures, letting go of habits, patterns, and things that are part of our lives because of someone else's influence, we begin to feel and allow what truly resonates with *us* to be what surrounds us, what fills our days and what we move towards.

We slowly start to experience more pure joy in more moments of our days. We feel the heart lighten and get inspired. When we choose to actually embrace those inspirations rather than push them aside as impossible, impractical, etc., we come alive. They don't have to be big things, just real things that when we are in them let us be in joy that rises up like this pure little river of mirth like a child feels. And then we repeat again and again, listening only to that inner voice of the heart until we are in a flow pattern in our lives that allows no distraction away from that. That is what living in alignment with Self is.

Life can be a set of constant distractions that pull you away from that, but living is a commitment to listening to that, honoring it, and acting on it. What starts to happen is more and more joy, which brings more and more laughter, which brings in more and more Light, which brings in more and more knowing, which brings more and more aligned choicepoints, which brings more and more joy... the spiral continues to move upwards.

I bring this up because most of us haven't yet realized we are both the game maker and the game player of this reality. The closer we get to our unified state, the more clear this becomes and when we truly recognize that we are the ones writing the script, life changes radically. Manifestation becomes nearly instantaneous. Synchronicity becomes continuous. We start to own every single thing that is happening and that gives us real clarity on what we are magnetizing into our sphere to reflect back to us.

As Beings moving towards our full capacity to carry Light, we need to recognize that our light is dimmed when we are not in pure joy. A powerful Dragon named TiaRa once shared a great secret with me. Giggle therapy. When we are in full blown giggles, all of our cells are actually fully open and receptive to incoming Light. So when you are struggling to move through something or feel distracted from your Light, find something or someone that will make you laugh. Even 'generated' laughter is contagious and begins to percolate down to the depths where our own joy can start to surface and find its true eruption of mirth.

If our natural state is joy, our inherent nature is to be aligned to the flow and rhythm of the universe. We are moving into flow and away from construct. In 3D, construct is the basis, the operational system. It is task oriented. In 5D, which is joy oriented, construct becomes purely a support structure for flow. Doing vs Being. BEing is also not simply sitting in meditation or a state of bliss endlessly. BEing is not static. It is living in a flow of consistent action from the Heart; living from the core/centerpoint of intention. Once we master this and activate our Starphire, we move from BEing to Shining. (See Divine Human Blueprint section)

There is a helpful breathing exercise listed under healing practices to work on this.

In our natural state we are also 'creators'. Look at this simple drawing. Do you focus on the spaces or the lines?

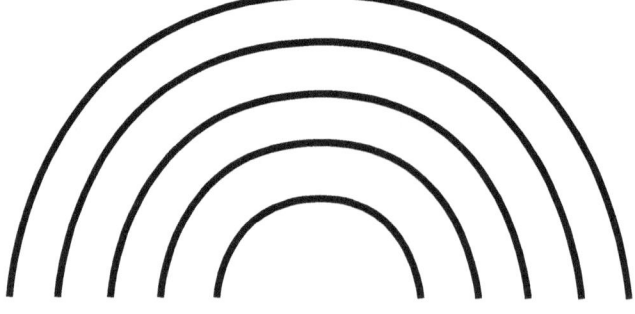

Our eyes naturally draw us to the lines. This is a representation of 5 dimensional layers. 99% of this is the space in-between the layers. The line or membrane separating those layers is the 1%. The construct we exist in on Earth is the 1%. We are actually believing that that membrane is the 99%!! When we move out of the membrane and into the space in-between, we move into the 99% of existence outside of our limited hologram. Within that, we are in a sea of potential where the process of creation exists. It is pure stillness until a desire rises within the heart of the Soul that then generates direction/light/creation. The field of potential holds all of the particles necessary for any creation and our heart generates the electro-magnetism to bring it into action or creation in which the particles pull together to match the vibration we have just sent out.

## CREATIVITY IS A MOVEMENT OF ENERGY FROM THE HEART SPACE THAT WANTS TO *GIVE*

# HEALING TECHNIQUES AND EXERCISES

## TO MOVE YOURSELF FORWARD

## HEALING OF THE INNER ASPECTS – CHILD, MASCULINE, FEMININE

*T*here are a multitude of resources in the world already for healing the inner child and you have most likely done some of that work already. What I would like to touch on here is the importance of recognizing that we have BOTH within us - a female child and a male child, regardless of the biological body we are in. This has been a big missing piece in healing work thus far. Similarly, the inner woman and inner man within each of us needs to be recognized, heard, embraced, healed if necessary and brought into each other's

presence. These 4 pillars need to come together as we complete.

With that awareness, it is equally important to be aware that we each have a womb and Hara space, which have typically been relegated to only women having wombs and men having the Hara as its power center equivalent. As you come closer to your union state, knowing this eases the confusion for men of feeling an energetic womb space in their field and for women of feeling something energetically apart from their womb space coming online that holds a great deal of power.

Revisit or start inner child and inner masculine/feminine work with this new awareness. If you don't have resources, simply begin in a meditation by calling forward one of these 4 and spending time with them. Ask what they need from you. Embrace them. Make them feel safe, honored, loved and respected and *listen* to what they have to share. Do this with each in turn and ask them for next steps to integrate and bring them together.

## BREATHING PRACTICE

There are a multitude of breathing practices out there. Most of them are about opening gateways for us to start going towards higher vibration. Working from the physical body up so to speak. This practice is about bringing the higher vibration down sequentially through our higher bodies to the physical level.

Syncopation: aligning to the pulse/breath of God which is anchored in us from our inception point to lift our lowest physical density into new form/alignment.

With intention sit quietly and begin to breathe, focusing on feeling the pulse or breath of God* deeply within you rather than on your actual breath. (*you could also consider this the underlying pulse of the Universe, like a heartbeat at the core of all that is)

First intend or allow your energy body to align with this pulse

Then intend or allow your emotional body to align with it. You will feel a wave of energy touch the heart center to trigger a physical breath response.

Next in allowing the mental body to align to the pulse, you will feel calmness, divinity, bliss descend.

Finally, allow your consciousness to recognize that the breath has shifted its rhythm to match this pulse.

Stay with this breathing pattern as long as you feel to. You are bringing your lowest vibrational body into alignment with your true central pillar frequency.

# HEALING DIS-EASE/ILLNESS/ MISALIGNMENTS/INJURIES IN THE BODY

**New methods with crystals:**

For years now, crystals have been employed to move and amplify energy in working with the energy and emotional bodies. It is now time to use them directly in realigning physical tissues. By introducing the silica crystalline structure template of the crystals directly to the tissue, it is like holding up a mirror of what it is supposed to look like for the tissue to not just heal via its old method, but replicate the template structure it is being reminded of. Our Human Divine Blueprint knows this structure inherently, but we have not been ready to align to it. Now that we are, bringing this into healing and repair of body tissues accelerates our full shift to silica.

**Methods with intention and visualization:**

Even holding the intention to align into our Solar Body or Divine Blueprint is a powerful enough tool to generate energy helpful to repairing or regenerating tissues in the physical plane.

One of methods is to 'listen' to the color/wave pattern of that part of the body in the unified quantum field. What does it sound,

look or feel like in its True state. We can then amplify that tone and/or color with intention into the part of the body in 3D that needs to realign itself and remember its true frequency/alignment.

Another method is the Perfected Human Healing Temple inside your DragonHeart or High Heart/LionHeart depending on your lineage. Spend time within the space where your soul seed resides with the intention to realign your physical tissues to the perfected human form (your Divine Human Blueprint) that was created at your inception point. By calling in your higher awareness of your true blueprint, you can begin to align as closely as you can with it.

You can work on a specific area of the body to feel the perfection of the tissue or bone and 'mirror' the geometric pattern within your perfected human form of that back into the afflicted part in the lower vibrational field. You can also visualize the harmony and alignment of the entire body into its divine blueprint.

Examples:

- with a broken bone, align to and mirror back the healthy bone structure within the blueprint

- a condition like diabetes, align to and mirror back perfect insulin creation

- illness or virus in the body, align to and mirror back the antibodies or perfected cell structure that can't be attacked

You can also do this with/for others, such as clients and family. The intention is to come into geometric countenance with your client or family member as you do so. This means aligning to their soul signature and blueprint by using yours as a bridge to connect into it. Your higher Self will more easily be able to call theirs forward than your lower self.

# INNER SPACE EXPANSION

Our vibrational increase as we move towards ascension comes in stages during which both our exterior physical aspect and our inner energetic aspects begin to shift. We become 'fed' or receive more and more through the inner space and so it begins to expand, gently moving us towards the full capacity and use of our Telepathic and Divine Communion bodies (see Section on the Shift of Lower 4 Bodies to Upper 4 Bodies) and away from reliance on the lower physical (senses), mental and emotional bodies as our main interface with our reality.

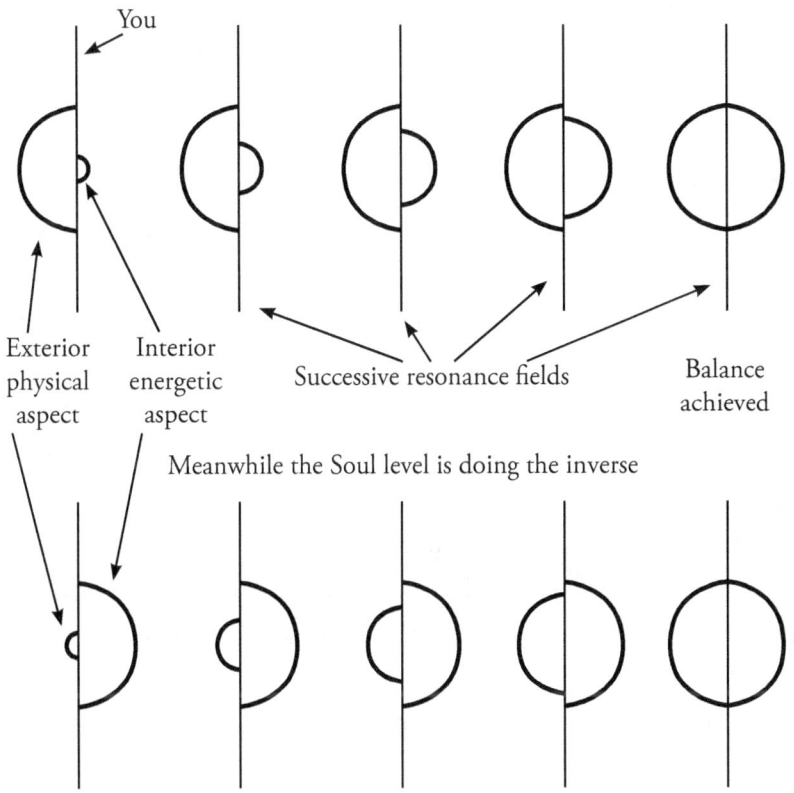

You

Exterior physical aspect

Interior energetic aspect

Successive resonance fields

Balance achieved

Meanwhile the Soul level is doing the inverse

A great metaphor for this process would be to look at the creation and ripening of a cherry. That cherry is being fed externally by the sun and so its outer 'physical' body expands, while at the same time its inner body is being fed and nourished through the ground, the water, and the nutrients being created through photosynthesis within the tree. When all is in balance, there is a beautiful, plump, perfectly ripe cherry.

Much like that our physical aspect on this side of the inner spaces gets fed by the external environment, while we expand ourselves towards that inner sanctum ('the spaces in-between'). Simultaneously, our Soul level aspect, is in its fullness within that space and working to expand itself towards our external physical space. It will expand into that to the lowest frequency bandwidth before 'matter' and that is where we have to be ready to merge with it.

Because we are at the dimensional density boundary, literally at the threshold of a dimensional shift, every subtle, tiny awareness of Soul level expands us into that new threshold. It is a subtle line to cross, but a massive step and shift. It behooves us then to spend time truly coming to know our full Selves, our unique Soul characteristics. One way we can do this is to move into a meditation with the intention to merge with our full Self. That would be whatever your first incarnation was when your Soul was created and you may not even be aware of that in this moment. You can open to that information also flowing in. Allow your true Soul level desires to rise up. Then, see if you can find the common thread that they hold. This will show you more about your true characteristics. Even recognizing the difference between the desires at Soul level to those at your personality level moves your perception point towards that higher threshold of vibration.

## WORKING IN THE BLACK LIGHT

The Black Light is equally as important to work with and in as the White or Christ Light which is what most start with. You can imagine the Black Light as an emptiness that you allow yourself to freefall into. Falling into blackness can bring up many emotions, particularly fear, hesitation, anxiety and also memories of scary things in the dark. It is important to feel each of these as they rise and allow yourself to continually drop further in as you feel and release these emotions, trusting you will survive it. Let the darkness embrace you. In contrast to the feeling you get in the White Light that makes you feel held or escorted into the unknown by hosts of unseen angels, let the Black Light be the hug that says 'just let go'. It is a journey into deep surrender... the freedom in falling without fear.

## PULSE POINT IN THE HEART

The Soul Seed sits at the center point of the heart. It is the piece of our energy that separated out from the heart of our Solar Body as we had the impulse to incarnate as human. Within this seed, much like in a seed that will become a tree or flower, the hand of Mother/Father God rests within it. Through this connection, pulses of unconditional embrace coming from the Divine are constantly being received, whether we are able to perceive or allow them or not. When we come into awareness and allowance of this Light within us, we reflect it back to God and to the light within each other, activating others to open to it in turn.

Part of our struggle in this ascension process is to truly move back into unconditionality. We might be considering ourselves non-judgmental, loving, open, accepting, etc., but I guarantee when you start to truly see your perceptions of others, we hold a LOT of judgment. Particularly with those we perceive as 'bad', 'criminal', the 'devil incarnate' or the like. The easiest to see this with involves more public figures whose influence has huge effect on humanity, policy, etc. We are equally judgmental of ourselves. Dropping the self-judgment helps us to drop the judgment of others.

As a big heart opening exercise, this is what the Emerald Dragon King shared:

Think of someone you have a hard time 'loving' or even accepting. See the person that you would cast stone or judgment upon. Then look at them through the eyes of the Heart until you see them regress back to the point in their childhood (this could even go all the way back to the moment of their birth) where they were Light; an innocent, pure child before all of their own trauma, false beliefs and patterns set in. Your own Heart will respond with a pulse generation of self-recognition out to them without bidding or intent. It cannot help itself. It changes their trajectory forward, but also takes you deeper into the Truth of who you BE. It allows you to truly see them from your core, which will shift your own vantage point with everyone you 'judge' from there forward. You will start catching yourself in small conditions or judgements with people all around you. And repeating this will continually open you to your true capacity of a magnificent open heart. You cannot pass through the Zero-Point Gateway if you hold any baggage. Judgments are baggage.

Jeemla, the Dragon King, is calling you to your greatness. Greatness in the higher realms is measured through the Heart. It is the basis of all governance systems, hierarchies and councils. Like fireworks, we can be duds or tiny intermittent pops or cracks of Light bursting forth. Or, we can be those that explode out of the shell and accelerate out to the edges of the sky to Light it up. It is time for greatness. It is time for the Grand Finale of the fireworks show.

> Greatness in the higher realms is measured through the Heart

# WORKING WITH YOUR CHAKRAS AS THEY GO SPHERICAL

Consciously feel each of your chakras in its spherical aspect (see Section Shift of the Chakras from Linear to Spherical) and "turn on" the electrical nature within them, which is their crystalline light, starting in the heart chakra and then let it run through each from there. First let it run 'up' and 'down' to the root and to the crown. Then, begin to feel them interconnecting and follow the more fluid path of the flower of life structure they are actually moving into. Feel the trust in your body. Feel the greater Light flow within your body.

This is "shining your Light" all the way down into the physical level. This Light, this electrical energy, is the lifeblood of existence, both yours and all of existence. Allow your own Remembrance of that lifeblood in order to connect to the living organism of the New Earth 5D field. It is a field that we become a part of; no longer parasitic, but symbiotic in our connection as we become the neural and electrical synapses, the communication system, etc. of that field that we are in co-creation of.

# MOVING INTO MULTIDIMENSIONALITY

This exercise will help open your field to its multidimensional nature.

Allow yourself to visualize a drop of water. Become the drop of water. Now feel that drop of water dropping into a larger body of water. Maybe you are a rain drop hitting a lake or a spray of mist hitting the river below…

Experience being the drop, the ripples that move out on the surface as you land, and part of the water under the surface all simultaneously. Move into each singularly as you need to until you can feel them all simultaneously.

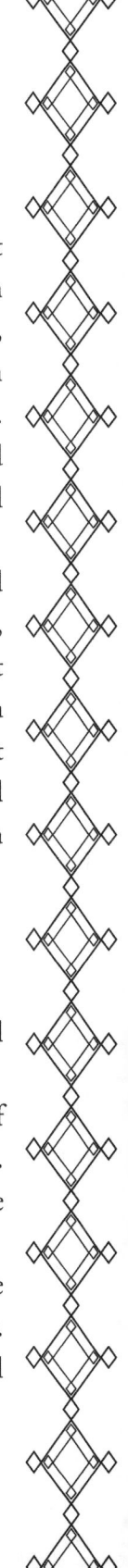

## MEDITATING IN THE EYE OF YOUR DRAGON

If you are familiar with the practices outlined in The Dragon Within, which was the first guidebook brought through to work with the Dragons in 2007, you will recognize the meditation to move into the Eye of the Dragon. This works with any dragon and you could probably try it with your own lineage if you are not Dragon at your core. This exercise involves the same practice but with the intention to move into the eye of your own Dragon (you at Soul level).

Go into quiet meditation, typically Dragons will find themselves in a cave. Pay attention to the environment you are drawn to.

As you center and move into a deeper state invite your Dragon (or higher Self of whatever form you BE) forward to be in front of you.

Ask to be brought into the Eye.

As the Dragon lowers their head to you with an eye presented, allow yourself to be drawn in through the pupil into its inner chamber. This is another access point of the Zero-Point Gateway.

Allow insights, questions, and whatever rises to flow through. Feel the communications streaming through the center of the heart space whether receiving or sending.

## DIETARY SHIFTS AND CLEANSES

Eventually, our bodies when aligned with their Divine Human Blueprint will be able to photosynthesize sunlight for energy and regenerate ourselves fully without the need for food or water. Until then, each of us has particular needs, so there is no right or wrong path with food choices. I do not believe that every Being that ascends has to be vegetarian, vegan or restricted in any way with what their body is telling them they need. However, I do believe that at certain stages of our process, we get an internal knowing of shifts that need to made either temporarily or permanently in order to access new heights vibrationally. I have been directed multiple times over the years to go vegetarian or vegan at certain times. I have also been directed to do fasting cleanses and to eat meat protein.

Most often in big energetic shift phases, our bodies need 'living foods that have drunk from the sun' to alchemize our cells into their capacity to do the same. This helps our stored cellular memory of our original blueprint to return to our natural capacity to alchemize all vitamins and minerals our physicality requires directly from the sun. Plants take in and store light for fuel. This resonates more directly with new cell demands and new frequency/structure as we embody more and more Light.

The key here is to follow your own knowing and be clear that it is your higher Self or guides directing your choices and not addictions, escapes, habits, false belief structures or other pitfalls. There are often planetary alignments that are global and affect the entire human collective, while other times your own astrological alignments will be reason behind an upgrade opportunity. When these happen and you get an impulse to eliminate certain foods, fast, cleanse, etc., it is important to follow them until that impulse shifts. For example, prior to specific December solstices, I have been clearly directed to go vegetarian for 3-4 weeks leading up to the solstice as that solstice has a gate or launchpad opportunity that I need to be as light vibrationally as possible for.

What you will discover on the path forward is that it is all about YOUR knowing and choice in every moment for everything you do. TRUST YOURSELF.

# MOVING AWAY FROM RELIANCE ON AND LIMITATIONS OF THE 5 PHYSICAL SENSES

The senses are truly the anchor that holds us in the 3D because they have been the only interface we have had with the world around us. They are a conceptual limitation of frequency. Just as the chakras shift from linear to spherical, so too can you work to move the senses out of a linear structure (visual stimuli come in linearly to the ocular nerve to be processed, sound comes in linearly to the ear drum, etc.) and ALLOW them to expand to a spherical experience in which you are able to experience both sides of them, or the full roundness of their true nature that takes in from all directions. This is aligning them with their 'clair' aspect within the energy body and thus taking a step towards opening you to a full signal of perception in which they are all woven together within the telepathic body. All of your 'clairs' have their openings within the 5th chakra, so around the neck and jawline area: clairvoyance (inner sight), claircognizance (knowing), clairailience (inner smell), clairaudience (inner hearing), clairsentience (inner feeling), clairgustance (inner taste).

## SOUL LEVEL BRAINSTORMING

Everything we are doing is trying to break free from the 3D bubble of constraint that we are held within. How do we break linear thinking to have a full paradigm shift? We have to do things differently. Even our creative process typically follows a linear pattern except for those few very artistically inclined folks who naturally find random to be a more comfortable space. For the rest of us, our brains like to be logical, to follow steps that take us from here to where we want to be in a specific step-by-step progression. When we are in the process of creation, because this is what we have learned to do here to reach a goal, this linear pattern can be hard to see, let alone break free of.

A beautiful Fire Dragon named Abraxinius brought in this process to assist us. It should probably actually be called heart-storming, because it cuts the brain totally out of the process. It moves us into creating, be it a business, a building, a coalition, a painting or a recipe. Creating from the soul space isn't just for art. With anything, we start by disconnecting the brain and all of its requirements or parameters that it believes necessary for the project. We then connect deeply into the heart, practicing the merge with our higher Self through the spaces in-between as described in the section Merging with Your Higher Self. We then allow the heart to bring things to the surface, be they colors, visuals, sounds or words from within the greater field of potential that exists beyond this level of reality.

These may seem 'unrealistic', 'impossible' or totally disconnected from what we put in as our creation intention. Let the soul work magic. This is where we make incredible advances or shifts in our own ability to open our own field of 'possible' both for ourselves and the collective as we let higher level inspiration come through. Things your mind could never have dreamed of, regardless of whether it is 'feasible' or not. Write it down or draw it.

Repeat this process several times before you allow the weaving to start showing you step 1. And don't expect step 2 to be next. It might work best to do step 5 next. It may feel Ike you are bouncing around within a project like a pinball. Trust it. My best teaching moments and most profound creations have come when I follow the impetus my heart and Soul level knowing is putting forward and put my mind, that wants to control things for everyone else's comfort zones in the back seat.

This applies with 'decision making' as well. When we don't know the way forward, our habit is to rely on structure, habit, patterns, and expectations. What we know. What we are comfortable with. What meets our expectations. But this is DO-ing vs BE-ing. When we come into heart presence, clarity comes of what our heart/Soul would choose. We then have to have the courage to make that choice.

## UPDATING THE SPACE AROUND YOU

There is great importance in aligning the vibration of your space to your new Higher vibration. Our surroundings enhance or detract from our energy field. As you expand, you will find your tastes in clothing, furniture, food, music and all kinds of things shift with you. It is vital to pay attention to these impulses and follow them. If it no longer resonates, why is it still around you? When you feel an impetus, for example, to change something (chuck it, move it, paint it), do not let the mental and emotional bodies overrule your heart knowing. All kinds of blocks to it will rise... 'but my mom gave me this', 'I can't afford more paint', 'it reminds me of'. These are strictly patterns based in fear and lack that you are breaking as you set yourself free and listen to the heart.

It doesn't mean you have to go get a new wardrobe or redecorate your entire home every time you shift, but you do have to listen to and notice the subtle things in your space that definitely no longer resonate with your vibration as it rises.

## RELEASING SOUL CONTRACTS AND SOUL BINDINGS

Most of us are aware of soul contracts we are engaged in with the people in our lives. We can meditate with intention to release or re-negotiate these. It is a fairly straight-forward process as long as we are truly ready to do so. It might first be necessary to ask to be shown any ongoing contracts we are unaware that we are involved in.

Soul bindings are more rare and a bit more of a process, mainly because we aren't necessarily aware of the level of contract we have been in with these. It is helpful to first even remember what these are. Soul binding is a more committed contract, much like marriage here on Earth. It, too, involves a ring (the inspiration for our ceremonies here?). When two souls choose to be bound, for whatever reason, they quite literally give an aspect of themselves to each other and become bound by a scribing of Light around each of their soul seeds. Choosing to be released from this, involves an 'unwinding' of that circle of Light and a re-insertion of what each gave back into the Self, obviously in agreement by both souls. This would involve a meditation calling both Beings forward, as well as a guide or Master that could unbind you unless you are capable of facilitating this on your own.

Because these contracts were done prior to incarnating into the Earth plane, they reside within our higher bodies (5th and 6th dimensional background bodies) and so are impossible to detect within the physical field of our lower bodies. We have to move into the spaces in-between to even find where the energy is housed and release it from there. In releasing it, a great void can be experienced which may leave you feeling untethered, agitated, or as if you have lost your center. In a way, you have, but it is giving you opportunity to become fully whole within this plane, filling that space with your own Light and coming back fully into yourSelf.

If during reflection with either of these types of contracts, you encounter cords, it is best to get clarity on who the cording is to/from, what purpose it is serving, and when it was placed. Family cords, like the silver cords with our parents, particularly the mother are often still in place, even though we have grown, moved on and possibly had families of our own. Be clear and loving in cutting all of them, even those with beloveds. All tethers in this realm have to be released in order to move through the zero-point gateway.

## COMING INTO ALIGNMENT WITH THE HEART'S DESIRES

When we are asked to express our heart's desires, most would either not be able to answer right away or would rattle off the list of

'dreams' we have on the back burner. The 3D realm has not allowed us to be in full expression and living in flow with our heart's true desires because of its demands, external expectations and rules of engagement. We are severely crippled trying to move towards a 5th-dimensional reality that is created and exists purely because of the flow of creative expression from the heart; the energy that flows out of pure joy as our Soul is inspired to express or experience something. We have forgotten how to even hear or know what the heart is longing for in every moment.

Our starting point then is to begin listening to what the heart wants moment to moment. Because of our routines, calendars, appointments, habits, duties... the schedule of our lives... we only let that happen when all else is done or maybe on the weekends or the end of the workday. This has to stop. When we realize that not only our participation in it, but the entire New Earth field is being created with every heart seed we make manifest, we will see how important it is to start listening. If every action we take is not motivated and driven by the heart, we cannot fully align to the higher reality field and it cannot come into Being. WE are creating the New Earth field. It is our heart creations that are populating and expanding it. The energetic structure is there. It is up to us to move into it just like moving into a new house. We can only furnish it with things absolutely inspired by our deepest heart. Just imagine how beautiful of a place that is to reside in!

Start by looking at all of the small things you do in a morning or a day. Then recognize whether each item on that list is being done out of 'duty' or pure joy because it is exactly what you want to do in that moment. What are the reasons you do each of these? Here are some examples to get you started, but your list will be much longer:

- ○ feeding the dog
- ○ brushing your teeth
- ○ mowing the lawn
- ○ working on a business project

- ○ heading out for an appointment
- ○ cooking for yourself or your family
- ○ cleaning the bathroom or the car
- ○ having lunch with a friend

This isn't about reproaching ourselves for the way we live, but about becoming more perceptive and more honest with ourselves about the why behind every action we take. Moving into a fifth-dimensional perspective is truly about shifting everything to the central pillar of the heart. What is our motivation for action? If the action is not heart-inspired, can it lie undone until the heart does desire it? If the heart never desires it, does it need to be part of our life?

What if I didn't jump up and brush my teeth right away out of habit? What if I waited until I really felt like it? The energetic component of the act would shift to a more aligned response not only from the teeth receiving the love being given, but I would be much more present and joyous while doing so. I would be giving to myself and that tiny act boosts my own inner joy, which then inspires another act of giving maybe to my dog by wanting to feed him and love him or to joyously make breakfast for my family. What is received with each action truly motivated from the heart is a totally different vibration and energy that allows the receiver's field to respond from a higher place: higher nutrition is received in the food made, clients receive more in a session, those walking into your pristine kitchen cleaned in a state of joy walk into a field of heart expression that opens them.

What happens if I don't do those things that are my routine? What little voices pop in to scold me, manipulate me or try to push me to do them? These are also important to see for what they are. What belief structure are they coming from and where did that belief originate in your life? Do I feel guilt, shame, fear...? Each of us have different anchor points into 3D. Our beliefs about how quickly these energies (yes that is all they are - energies) can be released and recycled determine

our journey and our dimensional density 'location' in the spectrum. These anchor points are just polarized faces of our natural states of joy, trust, knowing and connection. Let them be seen and thus able to move out of our field. In starting to recognize what we do from routine, habit, duty or expectation, we also need to start paying attention to where we go on autopilot. That is the moment our heart went elsewhere.

Are you getting the picture? The world wants us to be responsible, reliable, consistent.. to do things in a 'timely' manner. We learn to be this way because we have to be on time, show up for work, be there for our families, etc. Living from the heart doesn't mean we won't do or be those things. It means we allow them to be done in the perfection of the moment meant for them. We allow Truth to be consistent. We have to train the world or more accurately help the world remember how to BE in that flow. 'Inconsistency' is the flip side of the perfection of the now moment. It is living in a deep state of TRUST of Self and the knowing of the heart. Let your heart show you how incredibly big and beautiful it is and

# The flow of the universe does not have deadlines!

how magically creative it is even with seemingly 'rote' activities of the day-to-day of existence. When you prioritize the heart, all else falls into alignment with BE-ing. There is no effort in BE-ing.

People have a belief that time is their master, but it is a 3D construct! It is a formatted concept. TIME is a malleable mechanism. It is not even a *real* concept. The flow of the universe does not have *deadlines!* You can actually turn time off or on. It doesn't have to be a part of your reality. You don't even know what can be created when you are in your mastery and vision what you are creating. Let's imagine that you really want to finish what you are working on, but you need to be at a certain market to get some produce you need for the dinner you want to cook for someone. You are trained to believe that you have to quit what your heart wants to do and that you can't have both. BUT, in allowing fear about not getting to the market by it's closing time, you are not allowing the field of potential to open around you and support your heart flow. Magic can surprise you as you get there to either find the market stayed open late for some crazy reason, or a produce vendor opened a stand across the street, or maybe even a friend calling from the market out of the blue to see if you need anything. The universe will conspire to support you when you stay in the open field of potential.

Reality is a blank slate in every moment. Can we actually align to that and allow it to be? When we create on it from the heart desires and intentions in full alignment to ourSelves, this is how the journey becomes/is *magic.*

## THE INVISIBLE BOXES AROUND YOU

Taking the exercise of aligning to the heart's desires in another direction, we get another level of clarity about the invisible structures that are keeping us stuck in this paradigm.

Start by listing all the 'roles' that define you in the world. Think of as many as you can: head of household, husband/wife, mom/dad, employer/employee, son/daughter, student, sister/brother, handyman/woman, friend/supporter, etc.

Now take the top 2 (you can come back and do the others later) and list ALL of the things you believe you are supposed to be doing or are responsible for in those roles. For example, 'husband' = mowing the lawn, providing financially, feeding the pets, repairing the car or house, driving on family trips, setting up the tent, etc.

Look at each one. Where did that belief or thought form come from that you should be/are that role and that those things are part of that role? (i.e. a parent, sibling, partner or ex-partner, peer, mentor, teacher, society???)

Now look deeper at each activity listed for that role. Does it bring you joy? OR when you connect to your True Self, does it 'resonate' or not?

If it brings you joy: is it a pure joy of doing it? Or the 'joy' of the energetic kick back you receive from doing it and thus you like it. Careful… that one indicates co-dependence.

If it doesn't bring you joy, rather than continuing to do this activity, locate where this thought form that it is part of your 'role' to do so is sitting in the body. It will pop up somewhere like a black mass or spot of tension.

Connect to your Higher Self, expand that heart connection and send a dart of energy straight into that thought form to break it up. That is *all* it is. Dissolve it.

With this new found clarity, allow things to start shifting towards true joy-based action as discussed in the previous section. For those things that need doing that don't bring you joy either allow the timing to be inspired rather than scheduled or forced *or* outsource them to someone it does bring joy. Both result in it coming together more easily and rapidly with fewer road blocks or complications.

## DISCOVERING THE NUANCES OF JOY

One of the key pieces in elevating our perspective point in this ascension process might seem counterintuitive. Intuitively, we want to keep focusing on the Light, the higher vibration and holding that. That is definitely important, but when we come to realize the game that 3D is, we will see the keys in going deep into figuring out that game… becoming lost in it. It is the nature of this level of reality and to get out, we have to choose to pull out of the game by playing from a higher level. At some point, you will be so close to merging with your Higher Self, that you will begin to see that you are both the player and the game maker simultaneously. That is an empowering moment of realization and will dramatically shift how you interface with this reality.

What is also a very interesting 'by-product' of this moment and our full merge into Self is actually how much more 'human' we become. In my own journey, I was fairly shocked to see the shift my human aspect went through as I got more and more merged with my highest aspect. I loved this planet, but was not in love with most of life here, frustrated with most of humanity, and really ready to live in a totally different reality. What I didn't expect was that because I am in full connection with that higher knowing and awareness of the true rules of reality, I found myself in so much more JOY in being human. It's as if I was able to finally live as we were intended to in alignment with everything around us. There is a deep joy now in the very simple, little things of what being human is, even though I have become my full Dragon Self. Another aspect of Paradox.

That joy is multi-faceted as well. Have you ever sat with the question of what joy even is? How do you experience it? Where does it reside or how does it express/move through your body? Joy can be very subtle or ecstatic. How many nuances of joy can you identify in your experiences of it? Do they all root back to the same source-point in the body? By uncovering where it's source-point in the body is, we are holding a magic key because we can shift every choice we make to source from that point. This moves every choicepoint into alignment with Joy.

The next phase then becomes the movement from feeling joy as an emotion to experiencing it as our true state. As an emotion, joy is still a densified expression through the emotional body. When it becomes our true state of BEing, we have no filters, no blocks, no

residue and ALL bodies feel it. It also indicates our state of full merge with Self and thus the ability to experience the true state of everything. It takes being in your true state to fully realize and connect with all Beings in their true state. A tree, for example, is always in its true state, but we haven't been able to fully connect with it because we weren't.

## MERGING WITH YOUR HIGHER SELF

Historically I have taught people to merge with their Dragon. You might not be Dragon, but the process is similar.

**Method 1:**

Start by imagining your Higher Self coming up behind you. (Dragon, Angel, Unicorn, etc.) You don't have to know what it is yet, you can just allow the energy field to present, which may give you insight. Sit with this allowing yourself to perceive as much as you can and clearly feel their full presence behind you. Then, invite that energy to push forward and overlay your bodies (energy, emotional, mental and physical) as you allow yourself to move backwards into it. Just sit with this allowing whatever unfolds and whatever awarenesses or insights to come in.

You may begin to perceive wings, hooves, talons, fur, feathers, garments, appendages like tails, protrusions like horns, expanded energy...

**Method 2:**

As you get accustomed to method 1, now move into allowing yourself to perceive where your higher Self energy is and invite that energy to move through the spaces in-between into your bodies, usually the energy body perceives this first and is comfortable with it. Work with this until you feel it all the way into the physical body.

**Method 3:**

As you get accustomed to method 2, now move into allowing yourself to perceive where your higher Self energy is and intend to move up through the spaces in-between into it; this is a vertical upward shift in vibration to where your Higher Self is, which you will definitely perceive energetically. It allows you to perceive more Truth of your Higher Self than Method 2 as you are able to maintain a higher vibrational field.

Next try doing Methods 2 and 3 simultaneously. This begins to bring cohesion of the layers together and really moves you forward in maintaining a merged state of BEing.

Finally, as you feel this merge state more and more, focus on bringing the fullness of your Light all the way down into your bones, which are the densest part of you, and radiate it through all of the tissues from there. The Diamond Dragon and the Angelics are great allies to assist this process.

A Master's Training is to become aware of our level of desire to be in a merged state. How often are we merging? Why might we be dragging our feet (or tail as the case may be) to do this consistently?

What happens when we merge is the movement out of 'static electricity' (noise) into 'ec-static electriicty'. This offers a new awareness of our state of Being and brings forth the paradox and deep Truth of the two sides of the coin that that we are now immersed in: stillness and the effervescent bubbling of creative life force.

Your power center is your creative core. Thus your true power is your creative force. You ARE creating your life! The journey is squarely on your choices in every moment.

## PERCEIVING YOUR HIGHER SELF

After working with Method 1 in the Merging with your Self exercise, you can try this if you are wanting to get more visual clarity

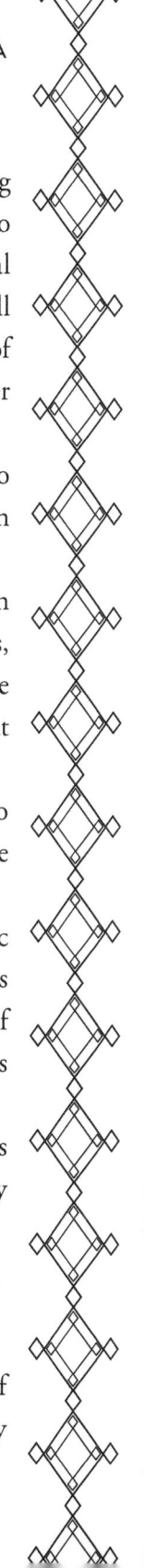

on what your Soul level Self expresses as. The Merging methods are very much focused on the energetic space, which can hold information for those with energetic acuity, but sometimes other perceptive aspects are helpful.

Again imagine your Higher Self coming up to stand behind you. Feel their presence fully as before, but this time rather than inviting them to merge forward into your bodies, feel yourself slowly turn around to face them. Allow your intention to be that your full telepathic field is open and perceiving anything it can. You may get 'visual' information that you don't actually 'see' clairvoyantly.

## RECOGNIZING YOUR PARADIGM

In this exercise, start by drawing two columns on a piece of paper. Label one column Mom (or whatever key female figure was in your life growing up) and the other Dad (or again the key male figure). Now, one at a time under each column, list the belief structures or patterns that you have around each of these themes and where they came from (which parent or mentor).

1. Money $$$
2. Power
3. Self-worth

Feel free to add other themes that feel key to you. These three are the foundations of the majority of our issues in the world and the way we move through it. They are the subconscious program that we are running. By allowing them to come into consciousness, you allow these structures to crumble because you finally see them. That opens up the space for your own True knowing about these themes to rise up and become your new foundation of choice and action in your life.

A great follow up to this is to sit with your Higher Self and ask for the Truth regarding each to come forward.

## ALIGNING TO YOUR PATH

What have you had visions of yourself doing?

- as a child, something you always wanted or could see

- in meditations or dream state

Try to be as detailed as possible about what you recall of these

Now taking one at a time, really sit with each one and examine why you aren't doing it.

- maybe it feels too big or too far out in the future

- maybe there are belief structures around money, worthiness, etc that are telling you that you can't have or do that

- maybe you can't see the first steps to get there, so you don't even move towards it or you compromise it to be less than your vision

These are all of your resistances that are surface level, earth-based falsehoods - belief structures - that you are letting sway you from aligning to your heart's knowing. For the big visions, they are also just the first layer and are covering up much deeper fears that may be soul level trauma. It is time to move through these in order to live out and experience all that you intended in coming here.

Let me share my own example. I had a vision years back of being onstage in front of several hundred people or more in what felt like a big auditorium. I knew I was teaching, but couldn't tell what it was about. It felt really big and I definitely felt like I couldn't see the steps to get there from where I was at in my life. I wasn't even teaching at the time or doing anything public. I had taught workshops and things before, so knew I wasn't daunted by that aspect. It definitely felt like a clear vision of my future.

Letting myself go deeper, an unexpected awareness arose from my Dragon aspect because I was focused on merging with my Higher Self and aligning to a deeper calling. I was stunned to realize that I was terrified of being in front of a large gathering because they would realize I was Dragon and I would be shackled and caged again.

## THE ASCENSION PROTOCOL

To the Earthly self, that seemed irrational and crazy. And yet, because it was soul level trauma still unreleased from previous dragon incarnations, it was affecting my current incarnations. All it took was seeing it to give me a clear path forward. Insight flowed of next steps, and even though it looked a little different, I moved into speaking globally via FaceBook, YouTube and Podcasts in live broadcasts and interviews. It may still align to be exactly what I saw, but that vision may also have been just a tool used by my guides and higher Self that aligned with the same energy that I would respond to. Not being too interested in social media at the time, I may not have understood or followed a visual of that type of audience.

## INSIGHTFUL CHECK-IN

I encourage you to do this periodically along your journey to see what remnants are still present as you progress. Draw 2 columns on a sheet of paper.

In column 1 make a list of all the things you value in yourself

In column 2 make a list of all the things you doubt or criticize about yourself

As your journey progresses, column 1 should start to grow and column 2 to shrink. These are indicators of your self-worth (heart center opening) and self-doubt (power center opening). It may also be helpful to see if there are still any things you don't think you deserve to have in this lifetime. This is another side of your self-worth. The Truth is that God wants you to have everything your heart truly desires. Do you believe you should have everything your heart desires?

This little story will start revealing to you the answer to that question. Imagine you have gone to the market and it is peach season. You adore peaches and want to buy some. You see 3 bins of peaches side-by-side and you are naturally drawn to the lush, deep golden, over-sized, perfectly ripe ones on the right. You then see the pricing signs.

The first bin are nice, light yellow, a little firm as if picked a bit early and have some blemishes. They are $4 per pound. Those in bin 2 are a bit bigger, a nice golden yellow and just about ripe. They are $8 per pound. Bin 3 that you were immediately drawn to are $12 per pound. Being really honest, which ones do you actually buy? Apply that awareness to every purchase or decision you make and see where your 'limits' are. Maybe you go for what you want with the smaller purchases, but don't let yourself have the bigger ticket items. Is there a dollar value or limit to your worth? And does it apply regardless of whether it is a purchase or a gift?

These are the very subtle belief structures that limit us from experiencing the greater reality that is the process of ascension. God wants you to have the $12 peaches if those are the ones your heart truly desires.

## VISIONING WITHOUT LIMITS

This exercise is about breaking out of all of our limits because we can see them *and* see beyond them!

List all you can think of connected to this question and all of the areas of your life listed:

What boundaries or boxes can you still feel around yourself in…

Where do you feel threads of constraint that hold you back?

- relationships: parents, children, lovers, friends, business associates

- financially

- the spatial size of the container you walk in and live in

- lifestyle

- spiritually

- any other areas that pop in for you

## THE ASCENSION PROTOCOL

Now envision how expansive you *could* be in these areas… what would that look like? How would it *feel* in your body to have full dominion (freedom) in that area? Be as detailed as you can.

Now envision your ideal life. You can do this in one area of your life at a time or merge them as a single vision. The goal is to be as detailed as possible in what you envision for yourself. Here are some trigger questions to get things moving.

What kind of home/work or business/relationship/environment relaxation are you in?

Starting with home delve into this level of detail with each area as an example:

Where is your home?

What style architecture and color is it?

How big is the property?

How do you get there - car, private jet, helicopter, canoe, snowmobile?

What make/model/color is this?

Do you have a driver or pilot or people that meet you when you arrive?

What is the name and/or number of the address?

What is around the home - trees, desert, pool, fountains, plants, landscaping, high rise buildings, beach?

What furnishing and color decor is inside?

What does each room look like?

What kind of showers or baths do you have?

What is the weather like there?

For your work or business:

What field are you in?

What days and hours do you work?

What is your ideal schedule?

Do you have staff, partners, a boss or co-workers?

Who is your client base? Try to see some of them.

What is the net income?

Do you travel with your work? If you travel, what does that look like?

What does your work space or office look like?

Are there windows?

What do you see from your work space?

Part of our journey here on Earth coming into our Mastery is remembering the incredible manifestors and creators that we are. We have had so many limitations put on us coming into this realm (that we allowed as part of the game/experience), that it is actually a bit frightening to realize what we are capable of when there are no more limitations. If the only universal rule is that we cannot impinge on another's free will, how different would our experience become as we take back that capacity to truly live in the field of possibility and potential? We don't have to be geniuses and build or invent in order to bring visions to life. We just have to know what our hearts truly desire.

## WHEN THE BELIEF SYSTEM SHIFTS, SO DOES THE EXPERIENCE

## CONTEMPLATIONS

What do you notice pulling on you as you move forward into the dominion, freedom and flow of 5D? Where do you feel limit or constraint, or just awareness of tethers?

What areas of your life need more balance. List top 3. (i.e. play vs. work, demand vs. allowance, trust vs. force, self-care vs. go-go-go)

These imbalances are connected to our ability to trust/surrender and to our self-worth. Would these be different if you were more conscious *daily* of who you BE?

# THE CONCERNS OVER THOSE 'LEFT BEHIND'

*N*ot all are choosing or ready for an ascension process. Those that are conscious or 'awake' are aware that there is a bifurcation happening that will eventually mean a full splitting of realities between 3D and the new 5D Earth. For some time now both have existed side-by-side as the new Earth field has been being created, opened and readied for our expansion into it. We are co-creators of that space with many in the higher dimensions that are helping with the structural parameters for it to operate. There is an 'unweaving' that will naturally occur between the two and is beginning as more and more are ready to move solely into a fifth dimensional reality.

With that awareness, there is often a concern for those that may be left behind in this process, many of whom are our family, loved ones, etc. First, as the paths bifurcate, it will not be a ripping apart but more like a gentle falling away. As higher frequencies expand into

the field, this creates space and the denser 'web' of third dimensional frequencies fall through it much like necklaces being untangled. This means it will be a gentle, natural process for all.

Second, it helps to recognize on a soul level that each soul and the path they are taking is already determined. There is no judgment or 'missing out', 'left behind', etc for those that are choosing to stay in 3D. It is simply that they are not complete with what they need to do in the school of Earth to move on yet. There is great love and compassion in that realization as hard as we may believe 3D reality may become to experience or 'endure'.

It is also really important to recognize that those that are ascending are predominantly the teams of Light here to open it as a possibility for the Earth plane. It is what will allow those that are first and foremost human at soul level (meaning their first soul level incarnation as a Being is in human form in this Earth Realm) to continue expanding vibrationally and come to greater connection with their Creator.

It is also very likely that many of those Light workers will stay close to the 3D plane and operate as guides and guardians for those in 3D, much like the higher dimensional guides, guardians and ascended masters that have assisted our process. Many of them are able now as we ascend to ascend themselves into higher formats and do something else in service. Have you considered that we are able to perceive these masters even though they aren't in our physical reality? We feel as close to them as we do to those around us physically. You may be one of those stepping into position as those ascended masters, but keeping your physical body!

Analogies always help the mental body grasp big concepts like this. A helpful one here is to imagine sugar dissolving in a glass of water. From outside of the glass, it seems to have disappeared, but *inside* the glass, it has moved into all of the spaces in-between of the water. Every sip is imbued with its sweetness. It can still be part of 3D for those that take a sip. If your perception is inside the water (5D), it is all around you, part of all that is. It is still there, not 'gone'.

## THE TIME IS NOW

You are now at the choicepoint. Both realities are present. Which are you choosing as your perspective? The elevator or magic door is NOT going to open up one day to reveal the New Earth that you can then step into. It is about your conscious choice in every moment to align to 3D or to 5D. Both are always present. The Web of Light is always around us, but we can continue to focus on the veiled, individuated bubble that we are in or move into the unified field of Light and become part of the signal. 'Uni' implies singular, but 'unification' is to bring the one into the many to become One. It occurs because of the completion of individuation and the desire to do so.

Everyone will reach this choicepoint, but will handle it differently. Imagine hiking up a mountain with a group. The group is halfway up and in order to summit there is a requirement to be in a merged state with your Higher Self for any steps forward on the journey. Some will take a lunch break. Some will stay at the halfway point. Others will choose to head back home to what is comfortable. Then there are those that have an internal drive based in a heart desire that pushes them forward. Their journey becomes a magnetic pull between their Soul and its seed anchored in the heart space pulling them forward.

The opportunity is at hand, although each will move through individually as they are ready. The 'Event Horizon' many speak of will be based on when you choose it to be. When you hold vibrational tenure - the ability to hold a certain vibration for a calculated period - the reveal can happen. Like a flip point, the reveal will happen instantaneously and all will be more vibrant around you. Gloriousness. Heaven on Earth is living in the relevant Harmonic! All the while, 3D will still be available like an app on your phone: once in the new

operating system, you can still choose to open it, reload it, enjoy it and then close it. It is your choice of where you sit vibrationally that determines what you experience. For example, you can choose to drop into 3D to fully experience ice cream if you choose!

To ascend, both desire and willingness have to be 100%.

Are you willing to risk everything to make the leap?

Do you realize you already did when you came here?

How many cycles has it taken you to wake up and see the veil or know it is there and that there is something beyond it?

# DRAGONS AND OTHER BEINGS ASSISTING THE PROCESS

# DRAGONS AND OTHER BEINGS ASSISTING THE PROCESS

*T*his is a glossary that shares some basic information about many lineages of Dragons and other Beings that may come into your field along your journey. It is shared mainly for you to have awareness of the many, many lineages (this list is certainly not all of them!) that are coming forward for humanity so that you might recognize them as they arrive or even call on them if it rises in your heart to do so. The majority listed are Dragon, primarily because that has been the most prominent field of guides presenting amongst my circle of clientele and students. They are also the key holders for most of humanity because of their role, so they are ready to work with all of us. Many of them and their lineages are laid out in the diagram at the end of the glossary as an easy reference tool.

## AndaRan Dragons

The AndaRans consist of a realm of Beings and Dragons that originally sourced out of a realm of stars birthing known as the Starlight Realm. It also 'birthed' the Rainbow Realms who have also sent many Beings to be part of the Legions of Light here in service at this profound time in Gaia's history. If you are familiar with Rainbow Dragons, fairies, all of the devic kingdom beings, unicorns, Pegasus, centaurs and most of the magical beings we encounter, then you are familiar with the energy of this realm.

Much like galactic Beings, the AndaRan Dragons use crystals to work with humanity. The difference is that galactic higher dimensional Beings literally insert their consciousness into a crystal skull (or other precious stone skull) like we insert consciousness into a human body. They use it rather than a body because they can maintain a higher dimensional platform and keep their knowledge intact to share with us. The AndaRans on the other hand use specifically AndaRa crystals and rather than 'inhabiting' the crystals, they send their heart energy directly into them.

AndaRa crystals are extremely rare and unique both in their discovery and their formation. They are a glass-like transmuted mineral complex high in monatomic minerals that exhibit profound metaphysical properties. The original location of their source is in Mount Shasta. There is a great story of their appearance and collection on 'Auntie Nellie's' ranch on the north side of Shasta. If you are called by these crystals, I encourage you to look that up.

From the Dragon aspect, I was shown an equally fascinating story of their creation. Wanting to work directly with humans and seeing that we were finally ready for such an interaction, the AndaRans worked through the cities of Light in the inner Earth planes. Telos under Shasta was the first location. Imagine one of these magnificent, vapor-like brilliant colored Dragons breathing mist or extending their talons into the mountain from the inner planes. That vibration coming into our elemental field created and left behind these beautiful 'crystals' of all colors as their talons and/or breath were pulled away. I have been told that other similar locations will surface as more are needed in locations also connected with inner Earth cities of Light, such as Bosnia and the Altai mountains in Siberia.

The AndaRan Dragons are extremely unique as well in that they are multidimensional bridges. They are simultaneously holding anchor points within 4D (the sound bridge), 7D (human angelic level) and 11D (cosmic angelic level) in order to mirror that multidimensional pattern for us to remember our own capacity to hold multiple dimensional bandwidths simultaneously. They hold these within the framework of the Love Lineage, so all AndaRans assist in opening the heart to greater depths and higher vibration. They also are amplifiers into other dimensions (like crystals amplify in this realm, but think bigger), mirrors of fluidity and support the pulling off of your limits. They literally want to 'take the lid off of your life' and assist you to reawaken the fluidity within your own Being to access all dimensional aspects of your own Self simultaneously. It is a teaching / gift/remembrance that is necessary for you to come into full *union* with Self.

When an AndaRan Dragon is calling you, you will feel drawn to a specific AndaRa crystal. They vibrate at a very high frequency already, but when there is one that is yours, your hand may literally begin shaking for you to recognize it. I was astonished the first time I opened a box of them sent to me as a gift as I was unfamiliar with them and my entire kitchen was vibrating! Each of the colors holds specific qualities but all will work predominantly in the heart space. They amplify like crystals do, but to a much higher degree. For those that are healers, the green healer AndaRas and their Dragons hold incredible expansion of the healing work as do the 'root beer' AndaRas that in my experience can amplify the projection of the healing greater distances.

## Arcturan Dragons

The Arcturan Dragons all present as DragonRider configurations and are 11th dimensional. The Arcturan system is a hub of activity and is considered to be the monitors or guardians of this side of the Andromeda Galaxy, which is the gateway to this universe. They usually present in a field of Rose Gold or as Rose Gold and/or Alabaster. These two earth elements were seeded by them and these two frequencies hold an energetic for a field of 'bi-directional resonance'. This assists us in moving back towards full multidirectionality. They also work directly with the White Dragon, who assists us with DNA activation, for our quantum expansion.

Our expansion into 5D can be compared to our birthing into the 3D realm. There is an inception point when our Soul chooses the incarnation, actual conception point and then a 'limbo' zone when we are energetically moving in and out of connection with the fetus or physical body continuously for months until about the last 6 weeks when we remain fully present. In a similar way, we have the inception point when we chose ascension, which may have been prior to this earthly life, the creation of our divine human blueprint that is our 'physical' body of Light accessible only from this plane, and now we are moving back and forth in connection to it until we can stabilize it. The Arcturans are one of the most helpful to work with to stabilize our field as we move into the quantum structure.

As a meditation with the Arcturan Dragons, you can visualize a sphere of alabaster around you, like being in an alabaster vase. Then allow rose gold to move in bands up and down the sphere. This will most likely begin to happen naturally as you send out a heart intentions to connect with them. You will notice the frequency around you begin to rise and sensations in the body of energy moving bi-directionally simultaneously and your awareness able to stay with this rather than needing to follow any singular direction with it. It may be uncomfortable at first, but stay with it and continue to work with it until you feel the presence of the Arcturan Dragon(s) with you in the sphere. Then, allow any work they want to do in your body field and/ or any messages that want to come in.

## Blueprint Architects

The Blueprinters are a massive team of collaborators from many systems specialized in blueprint technology. I bring them in here mainly so that you recognize them or aspects of yourself that may be part of that team. Just hearing a term like this can trigger awakening and memory that then allows you to expand further. These Beings may also come into your field as you approach your full merge and begin accessing your Divine Human Blueprint. They are both guardians and facilitators of the process.

## Core-Fire Dragons and Solar Lightning Dragons

Core-Fire Dragons exist within the core of any planet or system that will have elemental aspects. Within Gaia, they are in the deep interior of the planet within the molten core and they are connected to the formation not only of the elemental layers, but of the crystalline core of Gaia. They are often experienced energetically as fire salamanders when their energy densifies to connect with us. Once they show up, there is no going back in an ascension process. They only reveal when they are about to be released.

The Core-Fire Dragons work in tandem with the Solar Lightning Dragons as an ascension process progresses. The Core-Fire Dragons are like the energy of the Divine Masculine, the fuel, that when hit by the spark of the Solar Lightning Dragons, the Divine Feminine spark of creation, ignite an electrical impulse that moves along the central core bringing the Soul seat back into full crystalline connection with the Soul seed in the heart center and bringing the Wisdom, Love and

Power centers into full alignment anchored in the heart. This is on a planetary level for Gaia's centers as well as our individual level.

This activation allows the new circuit to begin running that is golden liquid plasma and runs like an infinity spiral around and through the three centers. This then begins to activate the bone structures, musculature, organs and tissues to begin the biological reformat towards the carbon to silica shift in alignment with the Divine Blueprint.

## Deep Earth Dragons (see also Opal and Black Fire Opal Dragons)

The Deep Earth Dragons, many of whom are present within the Divining with the Dragons Oracle Deck hold a vibration in the highest levels within the third dimensional plane. They are the guardians of Gaia's crystalline core and the deeper inner work and releases as we approach our crystalline activations. This is by no means an exhaustive list, but meant to give you an idea of some of those that you may encounter. In contrast to the Middle Earth Dragons who present in a more translucent, gemstone quality, they are typically opaque even though they hold a higher vibration. This is often how you can tell the difference between the two if you are not clear on the energetic difference.

Carborundum
Carnelian
Diamond
Jade (White and Green)
Jasper
Labradorite
Lapis
Moldavite
Obsidian
Rainbow Obsidian

Rainbow Selenite
Selenite
Snowflake Obsidian
Sodalite
Sugalite

## Elemental Dragons

In addition to the many ways the Elemental Dragons work with humanity as laid out in The Dragon Within, with more advanced healing modalities developing, these are other ways they can assist in those healings and clearings.

As a general rule, the elementals work predominantly with the following:

Earth Dragons: our physical body
Air Dragons: our mental body
Water Dragons: our emotional body
Fire Dragons: our energy/auric body

Call in the following dragons in alignment with these specific modalities:

Sound healing - Water Dragons
Light Therapy and Infrared Sauna- Fire Dragons
Steam and heat saunas (air compression) - Air Dragons
Crystal layouts - Earth Dragons. (The Crystal Dragons are also likely to present within these, but for those clients not ready for too high a vibration, the Earth Dragons are the best choice)

## Eternity Dragons and Infinity Dragons

The Eternity Dragons and Infinity Dragons hold the infinity pattern for us like a beacon or carrot to guide us forward. They are the pattern between polarized field (M and F separated) and unified field

(M/F in union). The looping 8 of the infinity pattern is like a Twin Flame energy that doesn't split between those two patterns. Their field holds the potential for systems and individuals to move from horizontal expansion patterns (always expanding but staying in the same vibration level or density) to vertical expansion patterns (those that bring about evolution into higher vibrational expansions). The Eternity Dragons are associated with the time vector of the Time-Space Continuum we are held within, while the Infinity Dragons are connected to the space vector.

## Flame Dragons

The Flame Dragons are 10th dimensional and access this realm via the void of the Nibiru/Solaris system. They are magnificent beings that stay as an emanation of light rather than densifying enough to take true 'form' because they have to maintain the intensity of their Light. Because they hold pure Light, they are guardians of specific processes and protocols that always involve purification of lower density systems. As such, they oversee shift completions on micro to macro levels, but especially of full systems like Earth is undergoing.

They come from many different realms and other universes and can be white, blue-white, orange-yellow, orange-yellow-magenta, magenta, black, neon green and many more variations. The color of their field is an indicator of their realm. Many emanate directly from the suns of their realms.

A useful meditation with the Flame Dragons:

Call out to the Flame Dragons and ask one to present to you. Take note of its color and any information this may provide you. Hold the following intention:

"I walk into the flame. I allow myself to be purified."

Then allow yourself to move slowly with this Dragon and walk through the Sun of each cell in your body, of each bodily incarnation of your Soul, of each planet and galaxy within your universe, and each multiverse your Soul is connected to. Feel the deep purification on all levels of your Being.

**Infinity Dragons: see Eternity Dragons**

**Lyrans**

The Lyrans are the new custodians of the Earth grids coming in to replace the Dragons who have been holding the grids since the creation of this system. The process of passing the batons is well underway. The Lyrans are mostly feline as Beings and the majority, but not all, move in an upright bi-pedal fashion as we do. That can be as Lion, Cheetah, Jaguar, Tiger and any of the species we are familiar with, but also many that are not within the Earth plane. They may be winged like the Golden Winged Lions. Their nobility are of the White Lion lineage, sometimes referred to as the Anahazi, and these Beings are holding an anchor of their frequency here on Earth embodied as such.

There are also other kinds of Beings within the Lyran system and lineage who originated within other systems yet have made Lyra their home. There are Dragons there, as well as Dragon-Lion hybrids. Many of these are here in service holding the bridge of energy between the two realms as the new Earth realm is constructed and the guardianship transfers.

There is a beautiful difference to comprehend between the DragonHeart and the LionHeart that helps us comprehend the positions that each hold for the Earth realm. The dragons have held the structure based on trines, the strongest form in geometry, that has existed since the beginning of the realm of matter in this plane of reality. They have always operated within a trinary system holding Wisdom, Love and Power as the core pillars. There is much more about this in The Dragon Within, which is a history and guidebook to work

with the energy of the Dragons. Being the guardians, they have held the keys to humanity's ascension journey. This book is a gift from the Dragons to humanity.

As the system moves into another pillar and a 4-based geometric system, we become aware of the 4th pillar that the Lyrans hold. Embrace. The simple, underlying key to the capacity to hold communal harmonic and transparence, which are the foundations of the 5th dimensional New Earth.

The Lyrans will present as you are ready to be aligned to the new grids. You may experience them coming in to replace your previous guides and guardian angels.

## Matrix Dragons

The Matrix Dragons are part of that which the multiverse ocean sprang from; the backdrop that holds it all. They are the spaces in-between other Beings that connect, hold, support and absorb. When in their presence, there is inherent awe because they are not only vast, but the antithesis of all that we know. They feel indescribable and simultaneously like something you have never known was there and yet have always known. You recognize it deep within your core.

## Middle Earth Dragons

The Middle Earth Dragons hold a vibration in the middle levels within the third dimensional plane. They are the the closest to us in vibration and present to work with us as we begin to really dive into our inner journey in earnest. They are eager to assist and hold great gifts for us, particularly the Emerald Dragons who hold Personal Truth as their core ray.

This is by no means an exhaustive list, but meant to give you an idea of some of those that you may encounter. In contrast to the Deep Earth Dragons who present in a more opaque stone quality, they are typically translucent or gemstone-like in appearance even though they hold a slightly lower vibration. This is often how you can tell the difference between the two if you are not clear on the energetic difference. Some of these are in the Divining with the Dragons Oracle Deck with more direct information and characteristics shared.

Amethyst

Citrine

Emerald

Garnet

Jacinth (Hyacinth)

Peridot

Ruby

Sapphire

Topaz

Zircon

## Opal and Black Fire Opal Dragons (Deep Earth)

Opal was the first layer of energy to come into form around the crystalline core. It then separated and opened the fractals into all streams or rays of consciousness into full 3D matter. Thus, opal carries all gems within it and is why it holds all colors within it. These Dragons can be envisioned like the top of the family tree of all of the Deep Earth and Middle Earth Dragons, as well as the energy opening the field for the lower density Black and White Dragon streams of energy to come through.

## Pleiadean Dragons

The Pleiadean System is a critical juncture within this universe. It sits at the midpoint between the outer edges of the 12th dimensional Andromeda system and the lowest 3rd dimensional aspects within the Earth system. There are 9 stars in the Pleiades. Most are familiar with

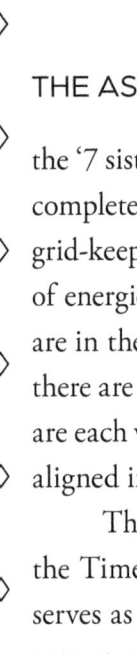

the '7 sisters', but not all are aware of the 'mother' and 'father' stars that complete the system. Each is associated with a specific Dragon as the grid-keeper of that point. These 9 Dragons hold a triple triangulation of energies that operates in a bi-fold capacity. The first triangulations are in the energies of the pillars of Love, Wisdom and Power such that there are 3 Dragons aligned with each pillar. The second triangulations are each within a dimensional sphere: 7th, 8th and 9th with 3 Dragons aligned in each.

This powerful alignment creates and holds the configuration for the Time-Piece Mechanism. It is a kaleidoscope-like mechanism that serves as a portal into the lower dimensions of this universe and is the gate at which our full Solar Body connection had to be severed. For eons, it has held the time-space continuum that we have adhered to within the current Earth system in balance. As humanity began its vibrational ascension, subtle shifts within the structure were finally able to be made by the Pleiadean Dragons as guardians of the mechanism. Those shifts have allowed higher vibrational tenure of each of the lower dimensional platforms, which thus allows the approach of our Solar Bodies through its gates. This is what makes it possible as we raise up into a 5th dimensional vibrational level to actually merge again with our Solar Body.

The 9 Pleiadean Dragons hold many keys for our reconnection to our Solar Body, particularly for those of Dragon lineage. This is because they hold the keys to activate your 9 Solar Body chakras. As you activate these in the merged space with your human aspect, you are pulling your human framework up towards your Solar Body to facilitate the full merge when all come online. As lined out here, they relate directly to a dragon's chakras, but I believe other Beings will benefit from the same work and become aware of the correlation to their own 9 core Soul level chakras along the way (or however many their species has).

As you work with them or experience them in your field, you will see that they are very etheric in nature, like vapor, and yet have 4 wings (imagine a dragonfly) that are perceivable. Their energies present in very brilliant, almost neon colors and very interestingly are associated with the energies of metalloids. Metalloids are a chemical element that has properties between metals and non-metals, or a mixture of them, in our periodic table, They typically have a metallic appearance, but chemically act like non-metals and have a crystal structure. No wonder they are connected to the full activation of our crystalline structure.

As a side note, for those unfamiliar as yet with the work in The Dragon Within, both the 5th dimensional Dragons of Orion and the 6th dimensional Dragons of Sirius are connected with metals, namely: gold, silver, copper, mercury, titanium and platinum. These metals are naturally 'lower' frequencies than the metalloids.

In this chart, you will have easy reference to the characteristics of each of the Pleaidean Dragons so that you will either recognize them or be able to invite them forward. You can also see their associated star, lineage and dimension (for their triangulations in formation), as well as color of their energy. An interesting point to note here that may help you remember them is that the 7D chakras align up the back of the body, the 8D up the central channel and the 9D out in front of the body.

| Star | Dragon | Lineage | Color | Dragon Chakra |
|------|--------|---------|-------|---------------|
| Maia | ShishanRa | Love 7D | chartreuse green | upper wing edge |
| Pleione | Sephalor Indrayam ('Sophie') | Love 8D | hot pink/ diamond | Soul Star (God Head) |
| Asterope | IlliaNa | Love 9D | magenta | high heart |
| Taygeta | ElastaRa | Wisdom 7D | turquoise | cerebellum |
| Atlas | PraderhanRa | Wisdom 8D | carbon/ diamond | Earth Star |
| Celaeno | Ingor-Dashnay | Wisdom 9D | indigo | high brow |
| Electra | SiRenAshar | Power 7D | lemon | lower wing edge |
| Alcyone | InguRa | Power 8D | vermillion | fire chamber |
| Merope | ArandaR | Power 9D | tangerine | sun (high solar plexus) |

The Double Triangulations:

Dimensional alignment:

7D Love = ShishanRa (Maia) Upper Wing, Wisdom = ElastaRa (Taygeta) Cerebellum, Power = SiRenAshar (Electra) Lower Wing

8D. Love = Sophie (Pleione) Soul Star, Wisdom = PraderhanRa (Atlas) Earth Star, Power = InguRa (Alcyone) Fire Chamber

9D. Love = Iliana (Asterope) High Heart, Wisdom = Ingor-Dashnay (Celaeno) High Brow, Power = ArandaR (Merope) Sun Chakra

As each Dragon's gifts are shared, please replace your own Soul lineage where the word 'Dragon' is. In sharing this information, as Dragons, they naturally focused on sharing it with and activating the Dragons on Earth, but I know they are ready to work with all who are ready.

The Dragons work in trines, the strongest geometric form. The Dragon holds 3 trines within its chakra system, anchoring it fully into Love, Wisdom and Power. A Dragon when in its True Form, fully aligned through its High Heart, Upper Wing and God-Head Chakra carries the greatest Love coming straight in from Source - Mother/Father God - and then powerfully can beam that out to all in its presence. This is why you experience them as so powerfully unconditionally loving. One of the greatest experiences of Love next to that of God directly.

Harboring the true power of Wisdom in its High Brow, Cerebellum and Earth Star Chakras, a Dragon has the power of knowing itself and its environment. It carries a connection to all of its soul's akashic records, a receiver to receive all information from its surroundings and an active center that anchors its frequency into wherever it BE. This is a two-way receiver as well, sharing healing, Love and Wisdom to wherever it lands, but also immediately tuning into the land it stands upon, giving it great insight and awareness.

## The nine Dragons of the Pleiades:

**PradherhanRa:** carbon/diamond, the patriarch and holder/activator of the Earth Star Chakra, which is about 12-20 inches below the feet, much further below on a Dragon

The EarthStar anchors the Dragon wherever it BE. This breaks the link to the Time-Piece Mechanism to pull us *out* of the time-space continuum. It is also our connection to the crystalline core of Earth which moves us into activation of our crystalline DNA and crystalline geometries.

He presents alternately between carbon and diamond states, like his carbon/diamond allotrope: same physical state, 2 forms. An inverted mirror of our one Soul with its 2 forms, lowest and highest, merging.

**Sephalor Indrayam (Sophie):** hot pink/diamond, the matriarch and holder/activator of the God Head or Soul Star Chakra about 12-20 inches above the crown of the head, much higher on a Dragon

"I hold space for shift and transition. I *am* the 8th dimensional bridge within the Heart of a Dragon. I hold each Dragon in my inner Chamber when they move through our mechanisms and birth themselves into the Earth plane. The 8th dimensional doorway is the greatest level of shift and transformation coming from other universes and realms in this one and so I an the Gatekeeper here to hold and nurture this process for each Soul that passes through. I shift in form through the transition zones. You will note this as mist and then rainbow. I am about subtle distinction within large transition. The oxymoron of the split second of stability in the doorway between 2 very different worlds."

So even though she activates the Soul Star as we reconnect to our full Soul Self, on the journey in, she is the Mother Figure that holds the space for us to transition out of our full connection to God and our Solar Body, which is through the core of the Heart (DragonHeart).

# THE ASCENSION PROTOCOL

This is the beginning of the shift to our only connection to God being through the crown as we descend into this veiled reality.

**Ingor-Dashnay:** indigo, breathes a purple flame, the High Brow Chakra, centered in the trine created between a dragon's ears and nostrils and then connected like a diamond with its point directly into the center of the head (what we would consider the amygdala in a human)

The High Brow Chakra carries a connection to all of a soul's Akashic records. This is different than the records we have had access to thus far connected to all experiences within this Earth plane which are held in the Halls of Knowledge or our Akashic libraries. This includes *all* incarnational aspects in *all* universes.

**ElastaRa:** turquoise, the Cerebellum Chakra at the base of the skull

The Cerebellum Chakra carries a receiver to receive all information from its surroundings, much like a giant satellite dish. ElasataRa works to deconstruct our model of understanding or what we believe our reality to be.

"I am here to expand you. Your consciousness coming from Earth is very limited and as you begin to take steps toward higher dimensional living while in your current framework, your parameters need to be widened dramatically. For one, the realization must sink in that 5th dimensional experience (and beyond) is *outside* your current understanding of a time/space continuum. You are eager to go there and yet like traveling to another country with no research or preparation, you would undergo a dramatic culture shock upon arrival.

I am here to broaden your mind let's say, or in actuality, help you step *out* of its construct and into the quantum leap of what lays beyond it. If you imagine several sets of railway tracks, a good analogy would be that you will need to slowly shift onto the next set of tracks. You cannot see reality as it is within the old rail system.

This is something that will take some time and needs to be gentle and gradual as it can be a very uncomfortable journey for the physical body to undergo."

**ShishanRa:** chartreuse green, the Upper Wing Chakra, on the upper edge of your wing formation; if you are not a winged lineage, feel where it sits behind you in a similar location

"I use the thrust of the upper wing to powerfully push the depths of Love that I hold directly towards the High Heart to expand it exponentially in harmony with my sister Iliana."

**IlliaNa:** magenta, the High Heart Chakra, half way between the throat and heart about 2" in front of the sternum

"When I come in, you will feel the high heart crack open to a whole new depth (even if you have worked with it before and begun opening it). Bringing together the powerful dynamic of Love that my sister ShishanRa pushes towards the high heart with a thrust of the upper wing and the ancient wisdom of experience to love from my mother Sophie, the action of recalibrating the high heart space to the 9th dimensional frequencies is my gift. Sometimes things have to shatter in order to be realigned and reveal new potential."

**ArandaR:** tangerine, the Sun Chakra (High Solar Plexus), half way between the heart and solar plexus about 2" in front of the body

This Chakra aligns to your Highest will, adds power to the Fire Chamber and holds a direct alignment to the Great Central Sun.

**SiRenAshar:** lemon yellow, the Lower Wing Chakra, on the lower edge of your wing formation; if you are not a winged lineage, feel where it sits behind you in a similar location.

"I hold the power center in the lower wing, the thrust that ignites the fire chamber and allows it to expel with great force. The thrust that carries the dragon's breath and frequency far out in front of it, in some instances to the far reaches of universes.

I connect with ArandaR who activates the Sun Chakra (High Solar Plexus) which aligns to your Highest will and this center sends

an equal thrust inward towards the fire chamber to add its force to the expulsion for the Fire Chamber.

One might not consider a 'wing chakra' to be of much import, but when a dragon can't fly because of a misalignment or injury, they are not in their full power. Dragons rarely have misalignments in their chakras, thus we are the protectorate; those holding the frequencies as the DragonHearts wake up so that they can reactivate their full system."

**InguRa:** vermillion, the Fire Chamber; for non-Dragons this would be wherever your power center is focused

"I am from a lineage of Sun Dragons that carry fire with them. The reason fire can exist in any of the lower dimensional is because I tend its ignition point within the time-piece mechanism that houses the access codes and creative matrices for the elements that it is made up of. I work with my father, PraderhanRa (Wisdom lineage) who holds the codes for carbon and my sister ShishanRa (Love lineage) who carries the codes for oxygen creation. I (Power lineage) carry the codes for Hydrogen."

Once activated, breathing from the Fire Chamber is a powerful tool. It can be used to:
- incubate eggs
- activate or pass information/energy Into initiates
- fuel manifestations
- breathe life into creations
- activate geometries

## Primordial Dragon Mother

She is a massive 'black' energy within the creation matrix.

"I am the energy behind all things. You see me as Dragon because I hold all forms and that is the one your Heart recognizes. Others will perceive me differently.

I will hold space for your resting point, for you to drop into complete and perfect stillness. You are trying to reconnect to an origin point and all origin points exist within perfect stillness. The in-breath if you will, before the breath of creation erupts through it in waves of Light.

It is this point you must connect to, to be fully immersed/embedded within your origin point blueprint. I hold it because it is an extension of me, as are you. I hold all form within me."

She holds our blueprints within her. A useful meditation to work with her is to visualize all of your activated crystalline geometries cohesing into an inward spin. Allow yourself to spin inwardly feeling her presence and be absorbed into her field. Ask to be pulled to where your blueprint generated from and resides in order to align with it to the highest potential in this moment.

**Rainbow Realm Dragons**

The Rainbow Realms were co-created by many realms. Dragons seeded in the magic that is inherent within this realm. Beings within the Rainbow Realms have the closest genetic coding to humanity and the flora and fauna of Earth. This is why they have sent a greater proportion of Light Workers than other realms. The Rainbow Dragons hold the Living Library of the Holographic Universe, which is different than the 'Akash' or individual soul records. Within it, all is fluid and it holds the original blueprint as well as all that has/is/will exist. They are always connected to the crystal kingdom and all of its 'rays'.

**Solar Dragons**

Solar Dragons are the energy that births, sustains and energizes solar systems. There is a council of 12 Solar Dragons working to kick our sun into its 'evolution' of full electro-magnetic energetic output.

They are connected to the increase in solar flare activity and our transition to a new "power grid".

Because they rarely interact with us, they are usually mis-identified as Sun Dragons, but their energies are distinctly different. Be clear in perceiving which they are.

## Starlite Dragons

These Dragons reverse or invert the vibrational field of the atmosphere (Gaia's energy body) to keep the cosmos in balance.

## Sun Dragons

Sun Dragons are birthed from a sun. They exist within all dimensional realms as every level has its own sun. Their energy is very similar to Solar Dragons, but subtly distinct. Be clear in perceiving which they are.

## Unicorns

The Unicorns began appearing several years ago for many. Hailing from the 'Mirror Realms' and some from the Rainbow Realms, they are coming in to bring back the magic and assist at portals all over the globe for the 'immigration' to New Earth.

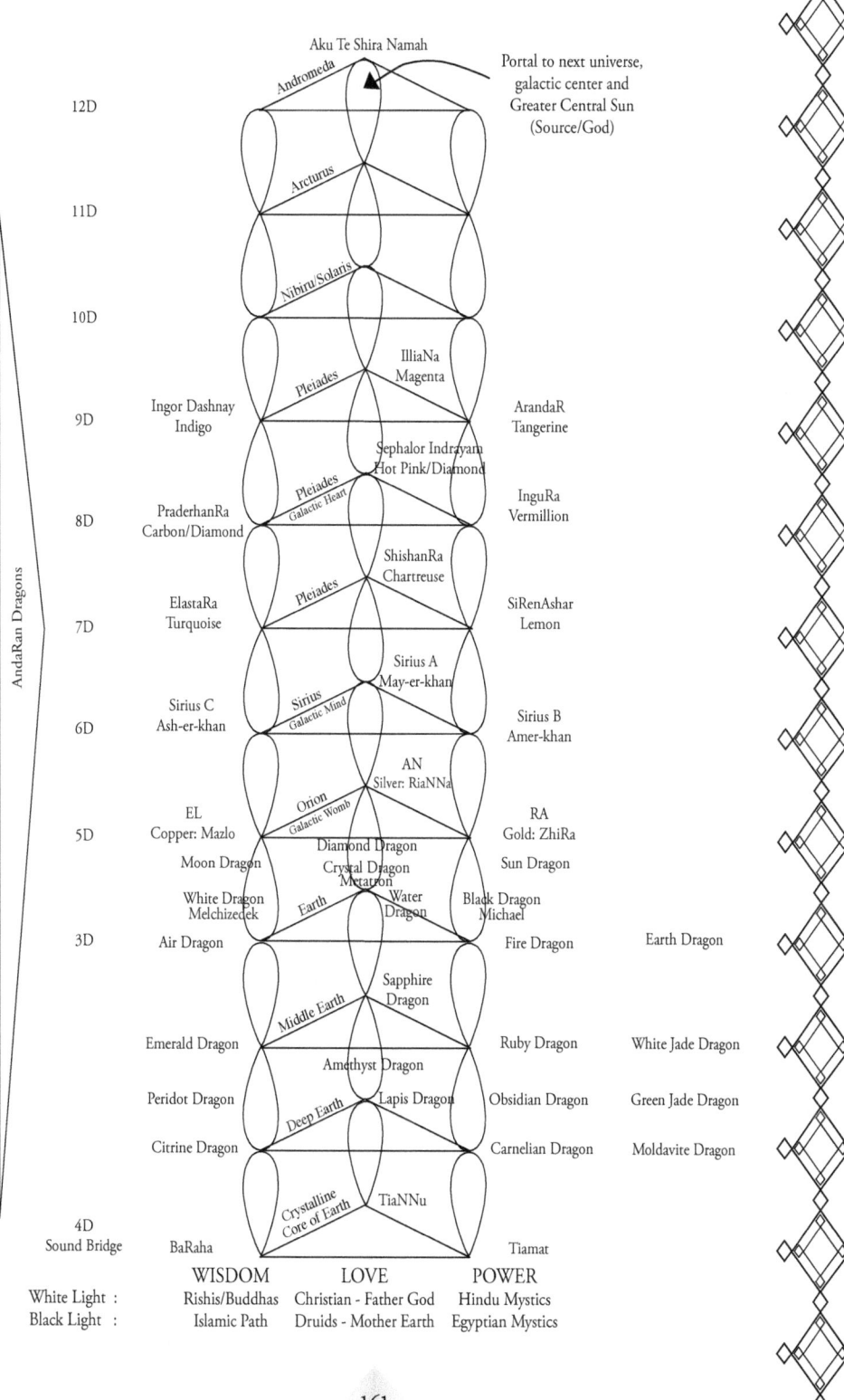

Aku Te Shira Namah

Andromeda

Portal to next universe,
galactic center and
Greater Central Sun
(Source/God)

12D

Arcturus

11D

Nibiru/Solaris

10D

IlliaNa
Magenta

9D

Ingor Dashnay
Indigo

Pleiades

ArandaR
Tangerine

Sephalor Indrayam
Hot Pink/Diamond

8D

PraderhanRa
Carbon/Diamond

Pleiades
Galactic Heart

InguRa
Vermillion

ShishanRa
Chartreuse

ElastaRa
Turquoise

Pleiades

7D

SiRenAshar
Lemon

Sirius A
May-er-khan

Sirius C
Ash-er-khan

Sirius
Galactic Mind

6D

Sirius B
Amer-khan

AN
Silver: RiaNNa

EL
Copper: Mazlo

Orion
Galactic Womb

5D

RA
Gold: ZhiRa

Moon Dragon

Diamond Dragon
Crystal Dragon
Metatron

Sun Dragon

White Dragon
Melchizedek

Earth

Water
Dragon

Black Dragon
Michael

3D

Air Dragon

Fire Dragon

Earth Dragon

Sapphire
Dragon

Emerald Dragon

Middle Earth

Ruby Dragon

White Jade Dragon

Amethyst Dragon

Peridot Dragon

Deep Earth

Lapis Dragon

Obsidian Dragon

Green Jade Dragon

Citrine Dragon

Carnelian Dragon

Moldavite Dragon

Crystalline
Core of Earth

TiaNNu

4D
Sound Bridge

BaRaha

Tiamat

AndaRan Dragons

| WISDOM | LOVE | POWER |
|---|---|---|
| White Light : | Rishis/Buddhas | Christian - Father God | Hindu Mystics |
| Black Light : | Islamic Path | Druids - Mother Earth | Egyptian Mystics |

# ACKNOWLEDGMENTS

*T*his work even though brought forth and woven together by me in this realm of matter, was truly a collaboration of many, many Dragons and Beings sharing their knowledge, their keys and their codes. Thus, the first big thank you goes out to all of the teams of Light Workers that have been a part of this.

Two Dragons in particular, that have honored me with their presence in my life via their human aspects for over 7 years need a special mention and thank you as the majority of the information brought through for this ascension process came in sessions with them. A deeply heartfelt and massive Dragon hug goes out to Jeff/Jeemla, the Emerald Dragon King, and Jeanine/Abraxinius, the feisty Fire Dragon.

Thank you to each of my core DragonHearts that have held a sacred circle with me to anchor and expand this information: Annabelle/EleeaRa, Chris/Ingor Dashnay, Diana/BeeshaRa, Leone/Anu'Shé~Ra, Long/Marvel AndaRan, Loretta/TiaRa, Manon/Nuriya, Robyn/AiKeeRa MaRaTani, Sam/Ardu NokTay, Tina/OomaRa Dayana. Our

monthly sacred space together is often what keeps me going amidst all of the shifts in play.

Thank you to Nicolás Alejandro Peña, the incredible artist who so beautifully captured the Dragons in the Divining with the Dragons Oracle Deck. His ability to bring to life my vision with this cover art was pure magic.

*H*ello. My name is Araya AnRa. Like you, I am many things; on a daily basis I wear many hats as friend, mother, sister, teacher, student, employee, business owner, healer— but each one of those is only a very small aspect of the tangible thread of Mother/Father God that each of us is. We are so much more!!

I have failed many times. I have been shattered many times. Each time, in the wake of healing, I find myself rising anew like a phoenix; each time reborn to a higher aspect of myself; one step closer to knowing and realizing God's perspective of who I truly Am. With every step in full surrender and a heart-driven desire to expand, my connection to everything beyond the physical plane expands. The clarity crystallizes of the next step, the underlying block, to whom or where I need to turn

for assistance. We all have pieces for each other. God's perfect Law of Attraction brings our perfect mirrors before us (as angry and ugly as they may seem). IF we are willing to look deeply into them, healing and shift can happen.

My real opening to myself began in 2002. Some inner voice was guiding me to quit my job and take time to go within. I was terrified, had a mortgage and lots of animal friends to feed, and not a clue how I was going to pay the bills. It was the most transformative time I can point to that started the journey of awakening for me. It was in the cloister of that cold, snowy Wyoming winter that I reconnected to my Self as a healer. It was as if I was remembering things I knew how to do long before being born into this body.

Exactly 9 years before that, I learned how to meditate at a Buddhist monastery in Southern Thailand and then set it on the shelf. Now meditation would become the doorway to knowing my guides and my future freedom. Talk about a powerful tool in the tool belt! The experience of learning the art of meditation was the 180-degree turn that has led to so many others since then. I began teaching and sharing meditation in February of 2003, a full 9-year cycle later, based on guidance during my own practice and a surrendering to the inner voice of Spirit trying to align me with my soul purpose.

Even with a whole new set of tools by 2012, I found myself shattered again. I felt like my life blew up after finally getting to a place where I was living my dream co-teaching workshops and giving sessions all over Europe. I lost my marriage, my work, my belief in myself… and found myself coming back to Reno, because that's where my family is, feeling like an utter failure and totally lost, and having to hold it together for my 3-year old son.

We can go the slow route. Or we can get launched forward. Both are appropriate at different phases of our journey. It took me four years of inner cocooning to recover and heal from the explosion. It is miniscule in the bigger picture of our journey to Love. And then,

I could again feel my guides tapping me on the shoulder and saying 'It's time. Let's get moving forward again.' So I started listening and trusting again. With two pre-arthritic thumb joints, I enrolled in a reflexology certification program. Ten sessions into the practicum, it became crystal clear why.

I found all of my energy work and psychic gifts that had been put on the shelf for a spell beginning to bridge with the physical work happening with the person on the table. I understood the new beautiful paradigm of the whole package being healed and shifted all at once. And I found my connection to the other side stronger and more clear than ever before, the energy flowing though me equally so and my desire to be in service to springboard growth in others that much greater.

From there the flow was in motion like the Truckee River in the spring thaw. Synchronicities just kept aligning for the next step and the next step and the next step. Thus was born Invoke Healing International. My small vision was going to be much bigger than I had expected! And now, it just keeps growing through my Facebook community and word of mouth.

So Who Am I? First and foremost I am a child of Mother/Father God on a journey Home. My personal expression of God is as a healer, a harbinger of change, a catalyst and bridge to removing blocks and finding greater Truth for each of the souls that feel ready to dive in. I am affectionately known by many as The Dragon Lady, as I have a unique relationship with the Dragons that allows me to guide others who experience the Dragons to understand them, connect with them and be healed by them. One of my greatest gifts though is being a galactic interpreter, which is what allows me to connect with so many individuals and Beings and be able to receive, translate and transmit the information wanting to be shared.

Other works by Araya AnRa
available at dragonwithin.com

The Dragon Within

Divining with the Dragons Oracle Deck

Mp3 Guided Meditation Collection with the Dragons

**Online Courses:**
Entering the Dragon Realms
Planetary Healing with the Dragons
40 Days in the Mirror
Meditation Basics

www.ingramcontent.com/pod-product-compliance
Lightning Source LLC
Chambersburg PA
CBHW061756120626
46550CB00005B/2017